"It is the depth and clarity of this account of the work of Melanie Klein that will impress professional analysts, psychotherapists, as well as the curious general reader. They will find readily accessible descriptions and explanations of many of the basic concepts of psychoanalysis – internal objects, splitting, projective identification, introjection, and pathological organisations, and learn how important processes such as mourning lead to changes in the super-ego which enable arrested development to resume. Even experienced psychoanalysts will be impressed to find old concepts presented in new ways, often amply illustrated with clinical material, sometimes from Klein and sometimes from Garvey's own work. This book is a major contribution to the definition of Klein's place among the pioneers of psychoanalysis."

John Steiner, training analyst, British Psychoanalytical Society, author of Psychic Retreats, Seeing and Being Seen, *and* Illusion, Disillusion and Irony in Psychoanalysis

T0386406

Melanie Klein

This important book provides a concise introduction to Melanie Klein and the key concepts and theories she founded, outlining their application to psychoanalytic technique, and explaining how her ideas have been further developed.

As Klein's ideas have opened the exploration of deeper and more primitive areas of the mind, they have led to extensive theoretical and technical developments across the world, in various schools of psychoanalytic thought. This book addresses Klein's early papers on her work with children and her extensions of Freud's ideas, as well as her divergence from them, highlighting Klein's emphasis on loving relationships in the mitigation of hatred, in children's overall development and in the drive for reparation. Examples from Klein's clinical work with children and adults are included to illustrate and illuminate her points.

Offering clear expositions of complex concepts and linking to more detailed sources of information, this book is important reading for all clinicians, trainees and students interested in emotional development and in the analysis of children and adults.

Penelope Garvey is a training and supervising analyst of the British Psychoanalytical Society. She worked with both children and adults in the NHS as a clinical psychologist before going on to qualify as a psychoanalyst. She works in private practice in Devon and teaches in the UK and abroad. She is one of the co-authors of the *New Dictionary of Kleinian Thought* (2011), co-edited with Kay Long *The Klein Tradition* (2018) and has recorded a short e-learning course, 'Introduction to Melanie Klein', which can be found on the website of the Institute of Psychoanalysis.

Routledge Introductions to Contemporary Psychoanalysis

Aner Govrin, Ph.D.
Series Editor
Tair Caspi, Ph.D.
Executive Editor
Yael Peri Herzovich
Assistant Editor

"Routledge Introductions to Contemporary Psychoanalysis" is one of the prominent psychoanalytic publishing ventures of our day. It will comprise dozens of books that will serve as concise introductions dedicated to influential concepts, theories, leading figures, and techniques in psychoanalysis covering every important aspect of psychoanalysis.

The length of each book is fixed at 40,000 words.

The series' books are designed to be easily accessible to provide informative answers in various areas of psychoanalytic thought. Each book will provide updated ideas on topics relevant to contemporary psychoanalysis – from the unconscious and dreams, projective identification and eating disorders, through neuropsychoanalysis, colonialism, and spiritual-sensitive psychoanalysis. Books will also be dedicated to prominent figures in the field, such as Melanie Klein, Jaque Lacan, Sandor Ferenczi, Otto Kernberg, and Michael Eigen.

Not serving solely as an introduction for beginners, the purpose of the series is to offer compendiums of information on particular topics within different psychoanalytic schools. We ask authors to review a topic but also address the readers with their own personal views and contribution to the specific chosen field. Books will make intricate ideas comprehensible without compromising their complexity.

We aim to make contemporary psychoanalysis more accessible to both clinicians and the general educated public.

Aner Govrin - Editor

Melanie Klein: A Contemporary Introduction
Penelope Garvey

The Unconscious: A Contemporary Introduction
Joseph Newirth

Guilt: A Contemporary Introduction
Donald L. Carveth

Melanie Klein

A Contemporary Introduction

Penelope Garvey

Routledge
Taylor & Francis Group

LONDON AND NEW YORK

Designed cover image: © Michal Heiman, Asylum 1855-2020, The Sleeper (video, psychoanalytic sofa and Plate 34), exhibition view, Herzliya Museum of Contemporary Art, 2017.

First published 2023
by Routledge
4 Park Square, Milton Park, Abingdon, Oxon OX14 4RN

and by Routledge
605 Third Avenue, New York, NY 10158

Routledge is an imprint of the Taylor & Francis Group, an informa business

British Library Cataloguing-in-Publication Data
A catalogue record for this book is available from the British Library

Library of Congress Cataloging-in-Publication Data
Names: Garvey, Penelope, author.
Title: Melanie Klein : a contemporary introduction / Penelope Garvey.
Description: 1 Edition. | New York, NY : Routledge, 2023. |
Series: Routledge introductions to contemporary psychoanalysis | Includes bibliographical references and index.
Identifiers: LCCN 2022051068 (print) | LCCN 2022051069 (ebook) |
ISBN 9781032105246 (paperback) | ISBN 9781032105260 (hardback) |
ISBN 9781003215714 (ebook)
Subjects: LCSH: Klein, Melanie. | Psychoanalysis. | Child analysis.
Classification: LCC RC438.6.K58 G37 2023 (print) | LCC RC438.6.K58 (ebook) |
DDC 616.89/17--dc23/eng/20221110
LC record available at https://lccn.loc.gov/2022051068
LC ebook record available at https://lccn.loc.gov/2022051069

ISBN: 978-1-032-10526-0 (hbk)
ISBN: 978-1-032-10524-6 (pbk)
ISBN: 978-1-003-21571-4 (ebk)

DOI: 10.4324/9781003215714

Typeset in Times New Roman
by Taylor & Francis Books

To friends, colleagues and students in Ukraine

Contents

Acknowledgements

I would like to thank Faber & Faber for granting permission for me to include in Chapter 5 an excerpt from Ted Hughes' poem 'The Blue Flannel Suit' published in *Birthday Letters* (1998). Thanks to Norton for permission to include in Chapter 4 part of the tenth of Rilke's Duino Elegies from Letters of R. M. Rilke, Trans/Eds B. Greene & H. Norton (1969).

Also thanks to Routledge for permission to reprint some clinical material in Chapter 6 that is taken from my chapter 'Separating and Splitting up' in *Freud's Splitting of the Ego in the Process of Defence* edited by Thierry Bokanowski and Sergio Lewkowicz (2009).

Great thanks are due to Elizabeth Spillius who helped me to think clearly, and to my husband Bill who taught me to write clearly.

Introduction

Melanie Klein was a follower of Freud and a radical thinker whose extensions of his ideas caused a considerable stir during her lifetime. Klein's way of thinking continues to cause controversy even though many of her concepts are now part of mainstream psychoanalytic thinking. Klein's ideas opened up new perspectives and in doing so opened up the possibility of further new discoveries. Her theories changed and developed during her career, and they have since been developed and expanded by psychoanalysts across the world. In this short introduction I aim to present her main concepts, to provide a sense of the way in which they evolved during her lifetime and to show some of the directions in which they have been taken. I hope to show the immense value of Klein's ideas to the understanding of emotional and cognitive development and to the way in which development can go wrong. Klein's thinking illuminates why we fail to co-operate with our better self, why we fail to co-operate with each other and why we go violently to war.

Klein's concepts are interdependent; to understand one you need to be able to have some grasp of the others. The twin problems of interdependency of ideas and the changing nature of Klein's ideas over time mean that I have found it impossible to conceptualize an ideal order in which to present them. To give a sense of the rationale behind the order that I have chosen, it is a mixture – at times the order is dictated by the chronology of Klein's work, at other times by an important theoretical development and at yet others the order is dictated by the chronology of

DOI: 10.4324/9781003215714-1

the emotional development of the individual. For example, the important concept of the superego appears in Klein's early work and is mentioned in Chapter 2 where I discuss her work with children. The concept is more fully explored in Chapter 5 where it is centre stage as a concept, where links are made to later developments in Klein's thinking and where its role as an anti-developmental force is set out.

Each chapter contains examples either from everyday life or from clinical work. Some examples are given of the way in which Klein's concepts help us to think about social and political issues.

Chapter 1 starts with a short biography of Klein in order to give a picture of the person behind the ideas, to place her in the politically fraught period in which she lived and also to place her in the context and history of the wider psychoanalytic community and the British Psychoanalytical Society.

Chapter 2 outlines the early development of Klein's ideas from her work with children, ideas that are the bedrock on which all her later theories rest. This chapter introduces the concept of unconscious phantasy and the idea of the internal world – the world in the mind in which imaginary figures full of powerful emotions interact with each other. This is the world that lies behind the way in which we see, experience and interact with the external world.

Chapters 3 and 4 explain Klein's overarching theory of the positions, the "paranoid–schizoid" and the "depressive" positions. While Klein wrote about the depressive position first, the paranoid–schizoid position is the first task of the ego, and for this reason it is described before the depressive position in order to provide a sense of how an individual might develop. Chapter 3 outlines the powerful anxieties of this early phase of life and the primitive defences of splitting and projection that are mobilized against them. These defences remain active throughout life in both the personal and the political spheres.

Chapter 4 details the complexities of the painfully difficult task of the depressive position in which the split parts of the self and the other are brought together into a whole. This task involves being able to give up and mourn the illusion of being an ideal self and of having links to an ideal other. The individual also has to bear the guilt arising out of his destructive urges. All being well, depressive anxieties are managed and the maturing infant or individual gradually develops a capacity for seeing reality for what it is, and for taking care.

Chapter 5 provides a look at the factors that interfere with the development from a paranoid–schizoid state of mind into a depressive one, described in the preceding two chapters. Some of the emotional forces that cause a retreat back into primitive ways of being or that hold primitive defences in place are described, as are the limits that these forces place on psychoanalytic intervention.

Chapter 6 is concerned with technique, in particular with the developments in technique and the use of countertransference, that have arisen out of Bion's concept of "normal" projective identification. Attention is given to Klein's views on the developments that took place during her lifetime.

I hope that this book helps to dispel two misconceptions. Firstly, the idea that Klein was a persecutor intent on unearthing the hostility in her patients, causing them painful feelings of guilt. Far from wanting to accuse or blame, Klein wanted to reduce pain and guilt. Her aim was to bring relief to those who suffered anxiety about their own aggression and who feared their own destructive power. Klein believed that hostile feelings of jealousy, envy and murderous hatred are normal and exist in us all. Klein aimed to widen and deepen the range of emotions that we can bear to feel and in doing so, to reduce our anxiety and the restrictions that we place on ourselves. In this way she hoped to increase our freedom to feel, to think and to act. She believed knowledge about the unwanted aspects of ourselves provides some protection against being unconsciously driven to action or imprisoned in inaction. Secondly, I want to dispel the idea that Klein considered environmental factors to be unimportant. For Klein the mothering that a child receives is crucial in modifying or in increasing destructive tendencies, and crucial also in supporting or failing to support the life instinct and loving feelings; in Klein's words:

Innate aggressiveness is bound to be increased by unfavourable external circumstances, and conversely, is mitigated by the love and understanding that the young child receives.

(Klein, 1959, p. 249)

Reference

Klein, M. (1959) Our adult world and its roots in infancy, in *The Writings of Melanie Klein*, vol. III. London: Hogarth Press, pp. 247–263.

Chapter 1

Biography

Melanie Klein was the youngest of four children born to a Jewish family in 1882, the same year as the German–Austrian student fraternities proclaimed their Waidhofer resolution, containing the chilling proclamation that "every son of a Jewish mother, every human being with Jewish blood in its veins, is born without honor and must therefore lack in every decent human feeling". Such was the threatening, genocidal world into which Klein arrived. Her father was a doctor, born in Lvov. The town was at that time part of Poland, but is currently part of Ukraine. In taking up medicine, Klein's father had gone against the wishes of his orthodox family who had wanted him to become a rabbi. Klein too was an independent thinker and is well known for not going along with accepted ways of thinking. This characteristic existed from an early age as is revealed by Klein's reply, when a child, to her father's demand that she eat up her food, "what was done a hundred years ago did not count today" (quoted in Milton, 2020, p. 65). Klein's willingness to make a radical departure from accepted ways of thinking was not an easy path to tread and she went on to cause a great deal of turmoil in the psychoanalytic world.

Klein's mother, born in Slovakia, was twenty-four years younger than her husband and has been described as a beauty, educated and witty. Klein's parents lived in Hungary and moved to Vienna just after Melanie was born. Her father was unable to find work there as a doctor and had to work as a dentist; he supplemented his income as the physician to a theatre. The family had little money and Klein's mother opened a shop in which she

DOI: 10.4324/9781003215714-2

sold plants and reptiles. The family fortunes improved when Klein was five, in part because the grandfather came to live with them but also because her uncle lent them money. They were then able to move to a larger apartment in a better area and Klein later reflected that she thought that as a young child she had been anxious about her family's poverty.

Klein's siblings – Emilie, Emanuel and Sidonie – were aged six, five and four at the time of her birth. It was an intellectual family and Klein describes being helped to read and do arithmetic by Sidonie and later being encouraged and helped with schoolwork by Emanuel. Sadly, when Klein was four, Sidonie who was only eight and greatly loved by Klein, became ill with tuberculosis, and soon died. In her autobiography Klein writes "I have a feeling that I never entirely got over the feeling of grief for her death. I also suffered under the grief my mother showed" (Milton, 2020, p. 66). Emanuel believed that Klein would do something great but at the age of twelve like Sidonie, he too became ill. He had scarlet fever that was followed by rheumatic fever which affected his heart, and the whole family were aware that he might not live longer than his twenties. Klein did well academically and attended the only school in Vienna that prepared girls for University; her ambition was to become a doctor. At this time Klein's father became ill and increasingly senile; gradually his health and the family fortunes deteriorated, and he died when Klein was eighteen. Despite his fragile health, Emanuel had started at medical school but he had then left to travel in Europe hoping to improve his health. Phyllis Grosskurth's (1985) biography of Klein contains letters written between him and the family that reveal the extent of their anxiety about his health and state of mind, and also their worries about money.

A year before her father's death Klein met Arthur, the man she was to marry; their engagement was long as Arthur needed to establish himself as a chemical engineer. Emanuel died the year before their marriage, Klein was twenty and wrote "the illness of my brother and his early death is another of the griefs in my life, which always remain alive to me" (Milton, 2020, p. 67). The impression from Klein's autobiography is that the experience of her family's suffering had a great impact on her and provoked in her a strong wish to be able to understand and prevent illness. Reflecting on her brother's death, Klein wrote:

> Here again I have the feeling that, had one known more about medicine, one might have been able to do something to keep him alive longer, ... but it left me with the same feeling that I had about my little sister, that many things could have been done to prevent his illness and early death.
>
> (Milton, 2020, pp. 67–68)

However, once she became engaged Klein gave up her ambition to become a doctor. In her autobiography she suggests that although she was up to a point in love with Arthur, she knew that she was making a mistake in marrying him, but her family situation of an ill and dying brother and a mother struggling to care for the whole family, meant that she said nothing to anyone and carried on with her plan. She married at the age of twenty-one and moved to Rosenberg, a Slovakian town in Hungary where Arthur had a position in a paper factory. Her mother came to live with them and stayed with them from then on. The family made many moves; moves that reflect the significantly changing political situation in Europe. Soon after her marriage, Klein gave birth to Melitta. She went on to have two more children – Hans three years later and Erich seven years after that. She became depressed during her second pregnancy with Hans and soon after his birth the family moved to Krappitz in Poland. Klein was particularly unhappy living in this small provincial town and to some extent her unhappiness influenced the next move, which was to Budapest, the capital of Hungary – a city full of cultural and intellectual activity. It was there that Klein read Freud's *On Dreams*; she was from then on convinced that psychoanalysis was the career that she wanted to pursue.

Klein's third child, Erich, was born only a month before the start of the First World War in 1914. Sadly, only a few months later Klein's mother died; she had never recovered from the death of her son. Klein wrote movingly in her autobiography about her grief at her mother's death and her wish that she had looked after her better. At about this time, Klein went into analysis with

Sandor Ferenczi, a leading psychoanalyst and a close colleague of Freud. Around the same time Klein heard Freud speak at a conference and was impressed. Ferenczi was to play an important part in Klein's development, he convinced her of the importance of the unconscious and he greatly encouraged her interest in exploring the mind of the child. In her autobiography she refers to him as having a streak of genius. Klein decided to treat her five-year-old son Erich; she went on to present her account of his treatment to the Hungarian Society and this led to her being able to qualify as a psychoanalyst and member of that Society. Analyzing a member of your own family is frowned on today but it was not unusual in those days. Klein had no supervision on her work, something else that would be frowned on today.

In 1919, to escape from the Communist regime, Klein moved with her children from Budapest to live with her parents in law in Slovakia. Her husband was at that time living in Sweden. By now her marriage had broken down and, after a year, encouraged by Karl Abraham, another of Freud's inner circle whom she had met at a congress, Klein moved to Berlin where she lived from 1921 until 1926. Klein's divorce came through in Berlin. Melitta studied medicine at Berlin University and it was in Berlin that, supported by Abraham, Klein began to develop a child psychoanalytic practice. Klein took on a number of children for treatment, but she found herself running into difficulties when she tried to analyse them using the classical Freudian analytic technique for work with adults – by which I mean expecting children to lie on a couch and to say whatever came into their minds. Klein found that the children were unable or too inhibited to free associate in words, but she was aware – and of course she had experience with her own children – that they could express themselves through play. In her autobiography, Klein writes about a time when she became frightened by the escalating anxiety of one of her child patients. She relates that she consulted Abraham and he advised her to go on with the analysis. She did so, the child's anxiety reduced and this convinced her that it was important to persevere in the attempt of uncovering the unconscious causes of anxiety. Anxiety, rather than drives or instincts, became the focus of Klein's attention.

Klein found that children's play was the equivalent to free association and dreaming in adults and she developed her 'play technique'. In her words,

> The child expresses its phantasies its wishes, its actual experiences in a symbolic way through play and games ... In doing so it makes use of the same archaic and phylogenetically-acquired mode of expression, the same language as it were, that we are familiar with in dreams; and we can only fully understand this language if we approach it in the way Freud has taught us to approach the language of dreams.
>
> (Klein, 1926, p. 137)

Klein's technique is still used today. Each child is given a box of their own that contains some small toys, for example small dolls that might make up a family, small animals including farm animals and wild animals, fences, string and some drawing materials. Sessions are at regular times, in the same room, ideally one that has running water. All this provides the child with figures who can represent important people in their lives and different aspects of their own feelings, within a setting that gives a sense of security and continuity. Klein thought that it was important not to see the child in his own home. This was in part due to the difficulty of working in the presence of ambivalent parents, but also, as she describes,

> I found that the transference situation – the backbone of the psycho-analytic procedure – can only be established and maintained if the patient is able to feel that the consulting-room or the play-room, indeed the whole analysis, is something separate from his ordinary home life. For only under such conditions can he overcome his resistances against experiencing and expressing thoughts, feelings and desires which are incompatible with convention and in the case of children felt to be in contrast to much of what they have been taught.
>
> (Klein, 1955, p. 125)

The importance of separating the analytic space from the patient's ordinary life raises an interesting question about remote analysis on the phone or on Zoom today, in which the patient remains in his own space, home, office, or car. Not only are patients sometimes inhibited by the actual presence of significant other people somewhere close by, but they may be inhibited by the experience of the analysis taking place in a location in which these other relationships are lived out. The analysis is not physically separated from ordinary life and certain resistances may therefore be less easy to overcome. There are many factors to be considered when thinking about the differences between remote and face to face analysis and this is just one.

In working out her theories, Klein combined the material from the play and drawings of her child patients with material from the imagination and dreams of adult patients and concluded that earlier versions of these imaginary scenes exist in the unconscious minds of the infant. It was from these scenes that she constructed her theories about what goes on in the infant mind. Just as Freud had extrapolated backwards from his adult patients to suggest early developmental stages in the child, Klein extrapolated backwards from the child to the infant.

Klein continued living and working in Berlin, but she continued to feel unhappy and in 1924 she went into analysis with Abraham. Abraham supported her work and wrote to Freud about Klein's amazing insights into infantile instinctual life. Klein gave her first paper on the technique of child analysis in Salzburg after which Abraham is famously quoted as saying "the future of psychoanalysis rested with child analysis" (Klein, 1932). Later, Klein herself, in her unfinished autobiography wrote "my work with both children and adults, and my contributions to psycho-analytic theory as a whole, derive ultimately from the play technique evolved with young children" (Klein, 1955, p. 122).

Ernest Jones, the founder of the London Psycho-Analytic Society, heard Klein speak in Berlin and he was impressed. He invited her to come to England to lecture on child analysis. Two other important figures from London, Alix Strachey and Joan Riviere, were similarly impressed. Alix Strachey was the wife of James Strachey, the translator of Freud's collected works, and she was in Berlin for her analysis with Abraham. Joan Riviere, an analyst, was there for the conference. Riviere was later to become a close friend, colleague and supporter, and she was to make a significant contribution herself to psychoanalytic theory. At around this time Klein spoke to Freud at a conference and later told James Gammill, a psychoanalyst who was in supervision with her from 1957 to 1959, that she was disappointed that Freud had not seemed interested in hearing about her work with children and disappointed too that she had not found much value in his comments. Nonetheless, this did nothing to reduce the high value she put on Freud's thinking. During this period of her life Klein had a love affair with a married Berlin journalist and some of their correspondence is contained in the Grosskurth biography.

Klein accepted the invitation to London and gave her lectures at the recently established British Institute of Psychoanalysis. She described the three weeks that she spent in England as one of the happiest times of her life. Sadly, Abraham died at Christmas 1925; Klein's analysis had been short-lived. So, when in 1926 Ernest Jones asked her to return to England, this time for a year to analyse six children, including two of his own, she agreed. Klein arrived soon after the opening of the London Clinic for Psycho-Analysis and, once in England, she decided to stay; she took on adult as well as child patients and her son Erich came to join her. At this time Anna Freud's (1927) work on the analysis of children was published in Vienna; it contained considerable criticism of Klein's approach and Klein states in her autobiography that she felt that Vienna had become an inhospitable place for her. Klein, now forty-four, settled for good in England and it was here that she continued to explore and to describe, in her many papers, the deeper layers of the child's unconscious. In these early years the differences between Klein and Anna Freud were debated – Jones gave a paper in Vienna, Riviere went there to present Klein's views and Robert Waelder came to London to reply.

In 1934, when Klein was fifty-two, her eldest son Hans tragically died in a hiking accident; he was only twenty-seven. His death added to the significance that Klein placed on the capacity to bear loss and the importance of the ability to mourn and to separate from the people whom one loves. Klein had a great deal to mourn, and she continued to suffer periods of depression. Roger Amos (2019), in his book on Klein's relationship to the

portraits that were painted of her, notes that the two that she dis-
liked captured her depression. He suggests that her hatred of this
being seen could be the reason that these were the two that she
rejected. Klein wrote about mourning and loss throughout her life;
these were themes that she worked and reworked with particular
attention to the complications of mourning the loss of someone
towards whom one felt hatred as well as love, a theme that had been
introduced by Freud in 'Mourning and Melancholia' (1917) and
developed later by Abraham (1924).

During these years running up to the Second World War, Klein
like everyone around her was keenly aware of the threatening
nature of events in Germany. Contrary to the view that Klein's
interest was solely in the internal world, she took a great interest
in the effect of world events on the emotional state of her
patients – the threat of war, the effect of the brief peaceful resolution, the effect of the outbreak of war and finally the effect of
the war itself. Claudia Frank, drawing on material from the Klein
Archives in her paper on Klein's references to Hitler, shows the
way in which Klein observed the interplay between external events
and the emotional forces within her patients (Frank, 2020). The
ideas discussed in this paper remain relevant and could be equally
applied to the current situation of Russia's invasion of Ukraine.
Klein saw that a powerfully destructive external presence stirred up
primitive violent feelings in her patients; a fear of the external threat,
and both excitement at, and fear of, the violent feelings within. Klein
observed the different ways in which these feelings were managed in
her patients and she saw that some patients defended against
acknowledging this aspect of themselves and preferred either to deny
the danger or to submit to an external power. Klein thought that, in
order to oppose Hitler, it is necessary to come to terms with one's
own primitive, violent sadistic impulses – the Hitler within. Opposing Hitler by out-Hitlering Hitler leads only to despair, whereas if we
recognize our own violent impulses we can control them and use our
aggression to stand up against destructive forces in the external
world. The importance of the recognition of destructive, sadistic
forces within all of us is a central theme in Klein's thinking as will be
evident in the chapters to follow. Roger Money-Kyrle, who was later
to become involved in the reconstruction of Germany in Berlin, was

a significant developer of Klein's ideas. He had analysis with Klein and earlier had been in analysis with Jones and then Freud. When writing about the causes of war in 1934 he put it vividly "We are like people who go about without knowing that their pockets are full of dynamite. The more we realize this the more likely we shall be to take all possible precautions" (Money-Kyrle, 1934, p. 132).

Klein continued to live in London except for a brief period during the war when she went first to Cambridge for a year, just before Freud died, and then to Pitlochry in Scotland. It was in Scotland that she analysed Richard whose analysis is documented in *Narrative of a Child Analysis* (1961). She was back in London in 1941 and for the next few years her ideas were hotly and intemperately disputed within the British Society. The arrival in London of Freud and his daughter Anna in 1938 added to the acrimony.

The main differences started between Anna Freud and Klein on their differences in the understanding of children and in the technique of working with them. Klein is famously reported to have quipped to someone "My dear we are all Freudian, only I am not an Anna Freudian". But the disagreements between them spread out to encompass the definition of psychoanalysis itself and the two camps, pro and anti-Klein, became increasingly entrenched in their positions. The British Society set up a series of meetings in which the disagreements were fully aired; these are recorded in *The Freud–Klein Controversies 1941–45* (King & Steiner, 1991). The meetings were painfully full of personal hostilities and many feel that the hostility went too far. Melitta Schmideberg, Klein's daughter who had trained as a psychoanalyst in London and was a member of the British Society, lined up along with her analyst, Edward Glover, on the side opposing her mother.

Jones later wrote,

> When, more than twenty years ago, I invited Melanie Klein first to give a course of lectures and subsequently to settle in London I knew that I was securing an extremely valuable recruit to the British Psychoanalytical Society. But I had no perception at that time of what commotion that simple act would result in. Until then, and for a time afterwards, our

Society was a model of co-operative harmony. For a time Mrs. Klein was given an attentive hearing and aroused great interest, soon – perhaps I like to think aided a little by my influence which was manifestly exerted in her favour – she began to win adherents and devoted followers. Before long, however, cries began to be raised that in the views she rather vehemently presented she was "going too far" which I think simply meant she was going too fast. Not that it was easy at first to detect anything radically new in these views or methods of work. The trouble was that she was pursing them with a novel rigour and consistent recklessness that evoked in some Members of the Society at first uneasiness and gradually an intense opposition. Other Members who championed her work with a certain degree of fanaticism found this opposition hard to bear, and in the course of time two extreme groups developed who between them vociferously, and therefore, easily restricted the quieter scientific endeavours of the cooler Members.

(Jones, 1948)

Joseph Sandler, a leading Freudian in the years following the Controversial Discussions, told Grosskurth that in his view the Discussions and their resolution were a great benefit to the British Society. She quotes him as having said:

Anywhere else in the world the Society would have split. There was something very special about the situation of the Society here, which kept it together. And this was a very good thing because being together made it necessary for people to sharpen their thinking in order to defend their particular point of view. It forced them to engage with those that held opposite opinions. It raised the level of British psycho-analysis enormously, I think. Constant debate strengthened the profession.

(quoted in Grosskurth, 1985, p. 407)

In the aftermath of the Discussions, Glover resigned from the British Society, Anna Freud resigned from the training committee of the Institute and directed much of her attention to the

Hampstead Clinic, and Schmideberg moved to America. A peace treaty was drawn up between the warring factions which involved the agreement that the psychoanalytical training of the Institute of Psychoanalysis be divided equally between an A group (Freudian) and a B group (Kleinian). A further group of analysts who did not identify themselves as belonging to either the A or B group were referred to as the 'Middle group'; they later came together as the Independent group. Donald Winnicott remained in the middle and refused to join the Independent group at that time, as he did not want to be part of a group, he wanted to be truly independent. He had been close to Klein for many years, but she had refused to take him on for analysis and he went to Riviere instead. Winnicott was taught and supervised by Klein; he was greatly influenced by her and was at one time a Kleinian training analyst before he moved away to develop his own ideas. At Klein's request, Winnicott analysed her son Erich and she wrote to thank him with the following words "I don't know whether I can convey to you how very grateful I feel for all you have done for Eric" (quoted in Grosskurth, 1985, p. 233). Klein analysed Winnicott's wife Claire. Winnicott remained loyal to Klein but he was critical of her followers, who he felt defended her ideas in a manner that set people against them and her, in a way that he considered Klein herself did not (Rodman, 1987). Klein only once referred to a paper of Winnicott's, and then only in a footnote (Klein, 1936, p. 297). The British Society continued to manage its internal controversies in the way agreed after the Discussions until the groups were officially disbanded some years ago. Theoretical differences and differences in emphasis and technique remain, as does rivalry about who is best, but at the same time many ideas are held in common. The ideas of each group now comprise essential blocks of learning for all candidates.

At the end of her autobiography Klein wrote that looking back at herself she could see that she had been spoilt and conceited and at the start of her career, very ambitious for attention, praise and admiration and wounded by criticism. Over time, and as she clarified her ideas, she felt that the ideas had become more important than herself. Klein seems to have ended her life with hope but also with some uncertainty about their survival. As we now know, her ideas have more than survived – they have flourished and have been extended and expanded across different schools of thought and across the world. All this was at some personal expense to Klein, which I think is alluded to in the chapter written by Jane Milton on Klein's late unfinished paper on loneliness. Klein was planning a book on loneliness, and she was intending to include comments and opinions from colleagues – Wilfred Bion, Elliott Jaques, Herbert Rosenfeld, and Hanna Segal and to bring in ideas from Winnicott's 1958 paper "On the capacity to be alone". Klein's notes at that time show her exploration of the need and wish of the creative individual to be alone with his own mind, but at the same time, the emotional difficulties that this causes.

> One cannot follow out an idea of one's own without doing it by oneself.
> …
> But distrust of the internal object not understanding or disapproving or grudging it comes in, which means an element of depressive or persecutory is bound up with it, this need to be alone.
>
> (Milton, 2020, p. 220)

Her notes explore too the tension between these feelings and ageing and death:

> It is well known that some people become more and more bitter the older they get. The resentment about the futility of their lives, about unfulfilled wishes and disappointments – going back to the earliest ones – takes hold of them. On the other hand there are people who become more mellow as they age, which implies greater tolerance and resignation. This tolerance and resignation is, as I found, linked with a longing for reconciliation – reconciliation with all the figures in their lives by whom they felt hurt or to whom they bore grievances. As always this applies to the earliest experiences as well. In the current situation it also means reconciliation with the fate of becoming old, with all the frustrations and disadvantages of age.
>
> (Milton, 2020, p. 224)

Klein made enemies in her life, she hurt friends and colleagues, and was hurt by them in turn. I do not know the extent to which she forgave her enemies or was forgiven but it would seem from the quote above that she wished for reconciliation. There is no dispute that Klein had a large body of supporters, that she inspired many during her lifetime and that her ideas continue to inspire thinkers across the world. In the words of Edna O'Shaughnessy, the editor of Klein's collected works, she was 'rare' (O'Shaughnessy,1986, p. 136). Her work is not always easy reading and the theoretical arguments set out in her early papers can be hard to follow. From her comment to Gammill after attending a talk by Bion, I think that Klein would not have wanted us to pretend otherwise.

> What on earth did (a certain analyst) mean when she said she understood perfectly what Dr. Bion meant to convey in his talk. I often have to read over several times the text of Dr. Bion's talks before I begin to grasp something of what he has to say. I have the impression that he is on to something new in psychoanalysis but it's no use pretending that it is easy and evident.
>
> (Gammill, 1989, p. 7)

I hope that this short introduction furthers understanding of Klein's main ideas, especially those that are not easy and evident.

References

Abraham, K. (1924) A short study of the development of the libido, in K. Abraham (ed.), *Selected Papers on Psychoanalysis.* London: Hogarth Press (1927), pp. 418–501.

Amos, R. (2019) *Portrait of a Life: Melanie Klein and the Artists.* Oxford: Phoenix.

Frank, C. (2020) On Melanie Klein's contemporaneous references to Hitler and the Second World War in her therapeutic sessions, in J. Milton (ed.), *Essential Readings from the Melanie Klein Archive.* London: Routledge, pp. 85–104.

Freud, A. (1927) *The Psychoanalytical Treatment of Children.* London: Imago, 1946.

Freud, S. (1917) Mourning and melancholia, *S.E.* 14. London: Hogarth Press, pp. 237–258.

Gammill, J. (1989) Some personal reflections of Melanie Klein. *Melanie Klein and Object Relations*, 7(2).

Grosskurth, P. (1985) *Melanie Klein: Her World and Her Work*. London: Hodder & Stoughton.

Jones, E. (1948) Introduction, in M. Klein, *Contributions to Psychoanalysis 1921–1945*. London: Hogarth Press.

King, P. & Steiner, R. (eds.) (1991) *The Freud-Klein Controversies 1941–45*. London: Routledge.

Klein, M. (1926) The psychological principles of early analysis, in *The Writings of Melanie Klein*, vol. 1. London: Hogarth Press, pp. 128–138.

Klein, M. (1932) An obsessional neurosis in a six-year-old girl, in *The Writings of Melanie Klein*, vol. 2. London: Hogarth Press, pp. 35–57.

Klein, M. (1936) Weaning, in *The Writings of Melanie Klein*, vol 1. London: Hogarth Press, pp. 290–305.

Klein, M. (1955) The psycho-analytic play technique: Its history and significance, in *The Writings of Melanie Klein*, vol. 3. London: Hogarth Press, pp. 122–140.

Klein, M. (1961) Narrative of a child analysis, in *The Writings of Melanie Klein*. Vol. 4. London: Hogarth Press.

Milton, J. (2020) *Essential Readings from the Melanie Klein Archives*. London: Routledge.

O'Shaughnessy, E. (1986) Review of Melanie Klein: Her world and her work by Phyllis Grosskurth, *International Review of Psycho-Analysis*, 14: 132–136.

Money-Kyrle, R. (1934) A psychological analysis of the causes of war, in D. Meltzer (ed.) (1978), *The Collected Papers of Roger Money-Kyrle*. London: Clunie Press, pp. 131–137.

Rodman, F. R. (ed.) (1987) *The Spontaneous Gesture: Selected Letters of D. W. Winnicott*.

London: Harvard University Press.

Winnicott, D. W. (1958) The capacity to be alone, *International Journal of Psychoanalysis*, 39: 416–420.

Chapter 2

Early Ideas and Early Work with Children

Klein's theories, derived from her early work with children, were inspired by Freud's theory of psychosexual development and its elaboration by her two analysts Abraham and Ferenczi, in which the individual progresses from the oral stage through the anal stage to the genital stage. In this theory, mental processes are conceptualized in terms of bodily processes. These early analysts were interested in the way in which we take experiences into our minds, what we then do with them inside and how we put them out. They conceived of a mental equivalent to "I should like to eat this" or "I would like to spit this out" and they used the terms 'internalization', 'incorporation' and 'introjection' for taking things in. The word 'projection' was used for putting things out.

Psychosexual Stages

Abraham worked with and had a great interest in understanding melancholic patients and he concluded that their difficulties are due to hostility towards their loved objects. This led him to subdivide the pre-genital phases into early and late; benign and destructive. In the early oral stage the infant wants to suck and swallow goodness and then in the later oral sadistic stage when teeth are developing, he wishes to bite and also to destroy the loved object. The following early anal stage also contains destructive urges; during this stage the infant aggressively expels his faeces. In the second anal phase the infant attempts to hold on to and conserve the good within. Abraham's subdivision adds complexity to the relationship between the

DOI: 10.4324/9781003215714-3

infant and his object and his and Freud's were the initial theories on which Klein based her thinking. Klein fitted her ideas into these developmental models while at the same time bringing forward, far earlier than had been suggested by Freud, the powerful emotions aroused by the oedipal situation.

> At a very early age children become acquainted with reality through the deprivations which it imposes on them. They defend themselves against reality by repudiating it. The fundamental thing, however, and the criterion of all later capacity for adaptation to reality, is the degree in which they are able to tolerate the deprivations that result from the Oedipus situation.
>
> (Klein, 1926, pp. 128–129)

In Klein's theory, the oedipal situation no longer arises from around the age of three or five years of age but is live from the start of life. 'Pre-oedipal' or 'early oedipal' activity became a central focus for Klein. Klein maintained that her theory was an extension of Freud's, but as time went on it became clear that her theory deviated significantly from his. She conceived of the young child as alive with jealousy, envy and hatred of the parent's creativity and filled with the desire to take possession of the mother and to banish and kill off the father and all rivals. Klein pictured these oedipal frustrations and urges as being fuelled by oral and anal phantasies.

Freud had described the way in which the Wolf Man's excitement and hatred at the parents' sexual intercourse was under the sway of his oral and anal drives (1918) and Klein similarly thought of children as being filled with phantasies about the primal scene; the content of which depended on the child's particular stage of development. In her paper "Early stages of the Oedipus complex", Klein (1928) turned Freud's component instinct 'epistemophilia', a wish and a drive to know, into an instinct in its own right. She described the Oedipus complex as involving early oral and anal sadistic epistemophilic wishes; that is the wish to get in, to know about and to possess or destroy the contents of the mother's body. The child then fears that his mother or the united parents will get in and attack the inside of his body. Klein believed that girls, aware of possessing a vagina, are particularly afraid of this kind of retaliatory attack. Klein's later papers, once she had worked out her ideas, are clear but the theoretical ideas contained in her early papers are often hard to follow. However, as described by Gammill, Klein did not want help to make them clearer:

> But when Jones offered once to rewrite one of her articles in the 1930s so that her thinking would be more clearly expressed, she thanked him and refused politely, saying: "it would be clear but it would no longer be me".
>
> (Gammill, 1989, p. 5)

Klein's vision is one in which the child has in his mind a whole world – an internal world – full of people or parts of people in relation to each other; hostile, loving and at times felt to be enjoying an orgy of continual mutual gratification. These activities provoke desire, jealousy, envy and great anxiety. Klein believed that boys as well as girls are particularly envious of their mother's creative capacity to be pregnant and give birth.

Unconscious Phantasy

Early in her career Klein put forward the concept of 'unconscious phantasy' in which bodily processes and sensations are accompanied by a mental equivalent. Klein's concept is much wider than Freud's, and the topic was one that was to cause considerable controversy. Klein thought that infants have an innate capacity to phantasize and that they are born with an unconscious knowledge of the body and bodily functions:

> The fact that at the beginning of post-natal life an unconscious knowledge of the breast exists and that feelings towards the breast are experienced can only be conceived of as a phylogenetic inheritance.
>
> (Klein, 1952, p. 117)

And she thought that phantasy activity occurs very early in life:

Analytic work has shown that babies of a few months of age certainly indulge in phantasy-building. I believe that this is the most primitive mental activity and that phantasies are in the mind of the infant almost from birth.

(Klein, 1936, p. 290)

Klein pictured the early infant as full of bodily sensations and instinctual longings (experienced as physical sensations) that are accompanied by unconscious phantasies. It was her view that the mental activity that goes along with physical sensation is fundamental, as is the phantasy of a physical activity that accompanies a mental activity. Although Klein described the infant's sensations and phantasies in words, she was aware that the experiences that she was describing are pre-verbal physical sensations rather than thoughts; words can be no more than an approximation of the sensation. Susan Isaacs, a member of Klein's inner circle of supporters wrote a paper on unconscious phantasy in which she described it as "the primary content of unconscious mental processes" and "the mental corollary, the psychic representative of instinct" (Isaacs, 1948, p. 81).

We do not know what goes on in the mind of the infant, but I will give some examples of the link between mind and body, and examples of phantasies of getting things out of the body and the mind which I hope will provide an idea of what might be involved in an unconscious phantasy. My first example is of a patient who told me that what I said was irrelevant. He said that when I spoke to him, he experienced my words as landing lightly on his lips, and he then spat them out. He showed me how he did this and explained that it was not difficult to get rid of what I said, as my words were insignificant and so they did not get in. A more chilling version of this is contained in Vladimir Putin's 2022 speech near the start of his invasion into Ukraine in which he said that the Russians "will always be able to distinguish true patriots from scum and traitors and simply spit them out like a fly that accidentally fell into the mouth".

My second example is of a child who attempted to banish an emotionally distressing memory. The child's stepmother told me that on one occasion when she was driving her stepdaughter and a young friend, she overheard their conversation in the back of the car. The friend mentioned the word 'divorce' and the stepdaughter immediately and forcefully told her that she must "never ever mention that word again". The friend replied "alright I will take that word out of my throat (she reached her hand as if to go down her throat) and I will throw it away out of the window (she took her hand out of her throat and threw it towards the window). The stepdaughter said, "its stuck on the window, you can't get rid of it". The stepdaughter had engaged with the phantasy, possibly not really believing it, that a word and not only a word but a bad experience could be eliminated if it was not mentioned. The friend went along with the idea and added the physical element of taking the word out of the body and throwing it away. The first child then acknowledged the reality that you can't get rid of it, you are stuck with the bad thing. Fantasy is one thing, but reality is another.

Many common expressions link feelings with bodily sensations; we say that we 'look daggers' at someone who we hate (we cut deep into them with hatred using our eyes). Being anxious is often described as having 'butterflies in your stomach', the Chinese say, 'sitting on needles', and for them the experience of feeling hopeless is described as 'falling into an ice hole'. In England we speak of wanting to eat up someone we love so that we can possess them and all their qualities. Ron Britton gave an example taken from the German press in which this phantasy was enacted in reality. A man called Meiwes killed, cut up and ate another man, after which he said, "since eating him my English has greatly improved" (Britton, 2018, p. 120). Miewes believed that he had incorporated not only his victim's physical body but also his mental capacities.

Klein pictured the infant as being engaged in powerful emotional relationships right from the start of life. She concluded that the infant's first focus is the mother and that all his longings, impulses and curiosity are focused on her body which is believed to be full of goodness, rival siblings and the father. Klein had the view that the infant treats the world as though it is an extension of the mother's body. In this way, his anxiety about the power of his own destructive urges towards his mother, along with his uncertainty about her capacity to survive them, is crucial to whether he then feels safe enough to explore the world around him.

The Fear of Destructive Urges: The Early Superego

Klein reasoned that the violent phantasies might lead to a fear of harming the mother, cause the child to become inhibited, leave him unable to be curious and lead to difficulties in learning. In an early paper Klein showed how Friz's difficulties with mathematical division are connected to anxieties of damaging his mother.

> He told me once that in doing division he had first of all to bring down the figure that was required and he climbed up, seized it by the arm and pulled it down … quite certainly it was not pleasant for the number – it was as if his mother stood on a stone 13 yards high and someone came and caught her by the arm so that they tore it out and divided her. Shortly before-hand, however he had phantasised about a woman in the circus who was sawn in pieces and then nevertheless comes to life again, and now he asked me whether this were possible … He then related … that actually every child wants to have a bit of his mother, who is to be cut in four pieces; he depicted quite exactly how she screamed and had paper stuffed in her mouth so that she could not scream.
>
> (Klein, 1923, pp. 69–70)

Klein's writing gives us many examples of children's play and behaviour; for example, she wrote about Peter, a young patient who threw a toy man down from the bed and said, "he is dead and done for". Klein suggested that the man represented Peter's Daddy. Initially Peter resisted this idea, but two sessions later he asked, "And if I were a Daddy and someone wanted to throw me down behind the bed and make me dead and done for, what would I think of it?"

In Klein's view the infant's oral, anal and oedipal desires drive the infant to want and to phantasize about the experience of getting inside the mother, taking possession of her goodness and killing off the rivals. Klein described a very fearful child, Rita, who was two years and nine months old. Rita had to be tightly wrapped in bedclothes at night. Her doll too had to be wrapped up and prevented from getting up "otherwise", said Rita "it would steal into the parent's bedroom and do them some harm or take something away from them" (Klein, 1926, p. 132). Rita also had the fear that someone (in retaliation) would get into her room and attack her genitals, which Klein understood in the following way:

> As I see it now, the fear of her mother attacking the 'inside' of her body also contributed to her fear of someone coming through the window. The room represented her body and the assailant was her mother retaliating for the child's attacks on her.
>
> (Klein, 1932a, p. 17)

Klein thought that, having made an attack on the mother, the child internalizes a harsh retaliating version of her or a combination of both parents.

> The attacks give rise to anxiety lest the subject should be punished by the united parents, and this anxiety also becomes internalized in consequence of the oral-sadistic introjection of the objects and is thus already directed toward the early super-ego.
>
> (Klein, 1930, p. 219)

Klein argued that the internal figure is an early version of the superego – "a terrible menacing super-ego" (1929, p. 203). Here Klein's theory moved away from Freud's. For Freud, the superego is the result of the working through of the Oedipus complex at the age of four or five when longings for the parent are given up and they are installed as authority figures in the mind. For Klein the superego precedes any resolution or giving up of infantile desires. In Klein's way of thinking the superego exists early on as a significant force within and is part and parcel of the oedipal drama. The first internalized objects, which in Klein's theory contribute to an early harsh superego, play an important part in Klein's theory of development and they will reappear throughout the course of this book.

The Internal World

Klein had the idea that the infant believes his experiences and sensations to be the result of a living presence inside who wants to cause pain on the one hand, or to provide a good experience on the other. For example, the infant might experience hunger as an ill-meaning intentionally malevolent presence inside him gnawing at his stomach. She pictured that the infant and all of us contain within us an internal world, full of objects and the relationships between them that we have taken in during the course of our interaction with others in the outside world:

> This inner world consists of innumerable objects taken into the ego (whole self), corresponding partly to the multitude of varying aspects, good and bad, in which the parent (and other people) appeared in the child's unconscious mind throughout the various stages of his development. Further, they also represent all the real people who are continually becoming internalized in a variety of situations provided by the multitude of ever-changing external experiences as well as phantasized ones. In addition all these objects are in the inner world in an infinitely complex relation both with each other and with the self.
>
> (Klein, 1940, pp. 362–363)

This idea is vividly illustrated in a paper by Paula Heimann who, like Isaacs, belonged to a small group of Klein's close supporters called 'the internal objects group' who wrote papers to explain Klein's ideas (Heimann was later to move away from Klein). Heimann's adult patient believed that she had small people running around inside her body pricking her with forks. Heimann explained "The memory-traces of psychical experience, past and present, are not static imprints like photographs, but moving and living dramas like never-ending scenes of a stage" (Heimann, 1942, p. 11).

Klein noticed that violence in children often alternates with very good behaviour and she became particularly interested in the separation between good and bad and love and hate. This separation can be seen in the play of her patient Erna, a small obsessional child who could not sleep, was terrified of burglars, rocked and masturbated and said there was something about life that she did not like. In Erna's play, polite children turned into devils and then into angels who never knew that they had been – or still were – devils.

> A teacher and a mistress – presented by a toy man and a woman – were giving the children lessons in manners, teaching them how to bow and curtsey, etc. At first the children were obedient and polite (just as Erna herself always did her best to be good and behave nicely), then suddenly they attacked the teacher and mistress, trampled them underfoot and killed and roasted them. They had now become devils, and gloated over the torments of their victims. But all at once the teacher and mistress were in heaven and the former devils had turned into angels, who, according to Erna's account, knew nothing about ever having been devils – indeed 'they never *were* devils'. God the Father, the former teacher, began kissing and embracing the woman passionately, the angels worshipped them and all was well again – though before long the balance was sure to be disturbed again one way or another.
>
> (Klein, 1932b, pp. 36–37)

The Life and Death Instincts

In 1932 Klein combined her ideas about the separation of love and hate with Freud's theory of the life and death instincts and from then on she explored the way in which the conflict between the instincts is played out within the individual and in relationships. Her particular focus was on the emotional state of the infant and the projective and introjective processes that take place in the mother–infant relationship. Klein's early ideas were later to be pulled together into her overarching theory of the two "positions".

The death instinct is a complex and controversial concept and it is described and understood in different ways. Freud put forward the idea of a death drive, a drive towards a state of nirvana, a dissolution of the self. Klein confusingly used the term when referring to destructive tendencies, self-destructive tendencies and to the anxiety aroused by the threat of being destroyed from within or of disintegrating and falling apart. Like Winnicott, Klein thought of the early infantile ego as unintegrated – in bits and pieces that are not held together and in danger of falling apart. For Klein the infant urgently needs to protect himself from being overwhelmed by anxiety and he also needs to organize his experiences. She had the idea that the early infant is full of terror of being destroyed from within; a terror caused by the death instinct, by the trauma of being born and by feelings of pain and frustration, such as the frustration of being desperately hungry and not knowing if food will come.

Projection

In Freud's theory the infant is described as deflecting out the death instinct onto the mother; that is to say, the infant turns the instinct of self-destruction away from himself and directs it at his mother in the form of an attack. Klein agreed but used the term projection, she wrote that the infant projects these feelings out into the mother or caretaker. Her use of the term projection includes the meanings of both projection and deflection; for Klein, the deadliness is turned towards/directed towards the mother and it is also attributed to her. The mother is attacked and is experienced as dangerous both because she might retaliate and also because the infant's deadliness has been located in her.

For both Freud and Klein, the infant also contains a life instinct; a desire and longing to be linked up and to make a loving connection with a loving other from whom love can be taken back in. In Klein's theory the projection of the life instinct is as vital as the projection of the death instinct. The balance between the life and death instincts is crucially important and the extent to which our constitutional endowment limits our capacity to benefit from experience is an endless source of debate. As you can see in the quote below, Klein thought both were important.

Innate aggressiveness is bound to be increased by unfavourable external circumstances and, conversely, is mitigated by the love and understanding that the young child receives; and these factors continue to operate throughout development. But although the importance of external circumstances is by now increasingly recognized, the importance of internal factors is still underrated. Destructive impulses, varying from individual to individual, are an integral part of mental life, even in favourable circumstances, and therefore we have to consider the development of the child and the attitude of the adults as resulting from the interaction between internal and external influences.

(Klein, 1959, p. 249)

Klein developed the idea that children feel overwhelmed by the conflicting instincts and emotions inside them and that they manage this conflict by projecting it outside into toys or into other people where it can be worked on or worked out in play. Anxiety about damaging the mother, rather than leading to the inhibition that I described earlier, can lead the infant to widen his field of exploration away from that danger and in this way develop his knowledge of the world. For Klein, everything and everyone is at base a substitute for the mother. "Symbolism … is the basis of the subject's relation to the outside world and to reality in general" (Klein, 1930, pp. 220–221).

Technique with Children

Klein's writings contain many examples of projection and lively examples of play. In an early paper "Personification in the play of children", Klein (1929) described the play of a young boy in which he switches roles with her and she uses this example in her third lecture on technique "Transference and interpretation" under the heading "Analysing deepest anxieties in children: John and the Lion". In their sessions, sometimes Klein was a lioness and at other times John was a lion. These lectures have recently been published in a book edited by John Steiner.

When John was the lion the analyst had to lie on the couch and pretend to sleep. It was supposed to be night time and John (the lion) would attack the analyst and devour her. My interpretation was that the child was actually afraid of being eaten up by her and that he was afraid of this because he himself, as a lion in his game, wanted to eat me up. But more than this he had as a baby wanted to get into his mother's room where she was asleep and actually eat her up, and these wishes went back still further to his wishes to devour her breast when frustrated in connection with feeding.

(quoted in Steiner, 2017, p. 58)

Klein explained that drawing attention to the denied aspect of the child's psychic reality brought those hostile feelings into his conscious awareness, and brought too his fear that his hostility could get out of control. She argued that her interpretation allowed John to take back into himself the devouring feelings that he had projected into her. She explained that in connecting his desires to their original objects – his mother and earlier still her breast – she was uncovering deeper layers of his unconscious. Klein concluded that John's anxiety reduced as he discovered that his impulses were not completely out of control and that his analyst was neither angry nor retaliatory. From this, Klein came to the conclusion that interpretations reduce anxiety in small steps. Klein thought that, as hate or destructive feelings diminish, love is released.

Transference

There was disquiet about Klein's use of the transference when working with children. Freud's discovery of the transference, that experiences from the past are applied to people in the present, had led analysts to try to recover their patient's buried history with the idea that bringing these memories into consciousness would provide a cure. The focus then moved on from retrieving memories from the past to addressing what it was that was being repeated in the transference, in the present. To this, Klein added the idea that enactments in the analysis also concern significant current relationships; enactments do not only concern the past. She argued that the powerful loving and hostile feelings existing in the form of unconscious and conscious phantasies/fantasies in the inner world are acted out in play and in relationships in the external world as well as in dreams. For Klein, the transference contains more than feelings towards figures from the past – it contains the interplay between these and current feelings towards those in the present.

Negative Transference and Modification of the Superego

Klein took the position that it is important not only to address the child's anxieties but also to talk to the child about his anxieties about her. When Klein first introduced her way of talking to children, one strong objection raised was that children do not transfer feelings about their parents onto the analyst because their relationship with their parents is still current; their parents are part of their everyday emotional lives. Klein disagreed as she thought that even young children contain an internal world of object relationships that colour their current relationships and these could be addressed in the transference. This disagreement was part of the ongoing dispute with Anna Freud and her followers and can be read about in Anna Freud's (1927) *The Psychoanalytical Treatment of Children*, and in Klein's papers "The psychological principles of early analysis" (1926) and "Symposium on child analysis" (1927).

Klein was very clear about the importance of talking to children about their negative feelings towards her as well as their loving feelings for her. She thought that it was only by acknowledging the negative transference, the child's hatred, fear and mistrust of the analyst, that the positive feelings could be secure. She maintained that the child's frustrations, anger, wishes to hurt or to control had to be talked about. In talking about these fears, Klein addressed the live feelings in the session. I want to emphasize that, far from wanting to accuse her patient, Klein wanted to reduce his level of fear and distress. She firmly believed that children and adults feel persecuted by the guilt of having negative feelings, that they and all of us are afraid of retaliation and suffer from feeling accused and threatened by an internal figure – a superego – that is frequently projected into others in the world around. Klein's idea is that someone addressing these feelings in a neutral non accusing way lessens the power of the internal harsh superego accuser.

James Strachey, a contemporary of Klein, made an important contribution to the thinking about technique in his paper "The nature of the therapeutic action of psycho-analysis" (1934). He put forward the idea that the patient attributes his 'archaic superego' to the analyst. This is a superego derived from infancy that is unrealistically ideal or unrealistically punitive. The analyst takes in the attributed superego and interprets in a way that shows the patient that he is neither ideal nor extremely punitive and that he is different from how he is seen. Strachey described the analyst as playing the part of the patient's 'auxiliary' superego. The patient will see the difference between the reality of their experience of the analyst and their expectation, and thus in a series of small steps the internal superego will alter.

> In the process of acquiring knowledge, every new piece of experience has to be fitted into the patterns provided by the psychic reality which prevails at the time; whilst the psychic reality of the child is gradually influenced by every step in his progressive knowledge of external reality.
>
> (Klein, 1940, p. 347)

Strachey made it clear that the interpretation that the analyst most fears making is the one that he should make, because this is where the emotional force lies. But in doing so, the analyst puts himself in danger of being attacked by the patient, who will strongly defend himself against the knowledge that he is being asked to take in. Strachey understood that it could be difficult for the analyst to make the necessary transference interpretation because the patient will direct his strong infantile feelings towards the analyst and so "in the analytic situation the giver of the interpretation and the object of the id-impulses are one and the same person" (Strachey, 1934, p. 289, footnote 18).

Disagreements

Klein's early papers caused a considerable outcry; not only was there disagreement about Klein speaking directly to children about their violent phantasies, but colleagues were shocked by the suggestion that little children, let alone infants, could be thought of as full of violence and that the violence was held to be inborn rather than in reaction to adverse experiences. The idea that small children and babies could have complex, sophisticated phantasies, desires and anxieties and be full of destructive urges was considered at best to be far-fetched. It still seems so to many today. These ideas did not seem so far-fetched to Wittgenstein, who was also brought up in Vienna at the same time as Klein.

> Anyone who listens to a child's crying and understands what he hears will know that it harbors dormant psychic forces, terrible forces different from anything commonly assumed. Profound rage, pain and lust for destruction.
>
> (Wittgenstein, 1929)

To Sum Up

Klein's work with children opened up a way of thinking about what is going on in the mind of the child and her theories brought focus to bear on the way in which early anxieties and the defences against them affect both emotional and cognitive development and also the structure of the mind. Klein's ideas provoked a great deal of interest in infant development. In time this led to the introduction of seminars on infant observation in which trainees visit a family with a new-born baby in their home for an hour once a week for one or two years. The trainee then discusses the observations that she has made on the interaction between the infant and his mother and others who are present.

Klein's approach to working with children has been enormously influential in the training of child analysts and child psychotherapists, in particular the development of the Child Psychotherapy training at the Tavistock Centre in London, which has in turn fostered training programmes across the United Kingdom and around the world. An excellent exposition of the complexity and range of child work undertaken by the Tavistock Clinic is given in Margaret Rustin's (2022) book *Finding a Way to the Child.*

As adults we all contain 'infantile' phantasies and emotions and these play a significant, and more often than not unconscious, part in our relationships with other people. Our present relationships are dominated by our past relationships. Whether or not primitive phantasies are present at birth and, if so, what form they take, it is impossible to know, but an understanding of the primitive phantasies in our internal worlds and their influence throughout our lives, is invaluable. Klein's ideas underline the importance of keeping in mind the power, force and enduring nature of early anxieties and patterns of relating.

References

Abraham, K. (1924) A short study of the development of the libido, in K. Abraham (ed.), *Selected Papers on Psychoanalysis*. London: Hogarth Press (1927), pp. 418–501.

Britton, R. (2018) The mountains of primal grief, in P. Garvey and K. Long (eds.), *The Klein Tradition*. London: Routledge, pp. 113–123.

Freud, A. (1927) *The Psychoanalytical Treatment of Children*. London: Imago, 1946.

Freud, S. (1918) From the history of an infantile neurosis. *S.E.* 19.

Gammill, J. (1989) Some personal reflections of Melanie Klein. *Melanie Klein and Object Relations*, 7(2).

Heimann, P. (1942) A contribution to the problem of sublimation and its relation to processes of internalization. *International Journal of Psycho-Analysis*, 23: 8–17.

Isaacs, S. (1948) The nature and function of phantasy. *International Journal of Psycho-Analysis*, 29: 73–97.

Klein, M. (1923) The role of the school in the libidinal development of the child, in *The Writings of Melanie Klein*, vol. 1. London: Hogarth Press, pp. 59–76.

Klein, M. (1926) The psychological principles of early analysis, in *The Writings of Melanie Klein*, vol. 1. London: Hogarth Press, pp. 128–138.

Klein, M. (1927) Symposium on child analysis, in *The Writings of Melanie Klein*, vol. 1. London: Hogarth Press, pp. 139–169.

Klein, M. (1928) Early stages of the Oedipus conflict, in *The Writings of Melanie Klein*, vol. 1. London: Hogarth Press, pp. 186–198.

Klein, M. (1929) Personification in the play of children, in *The Writings of Melanie Klein*, vol. 1. London: Hogarth Press, pp. 199–209.

Klein, M. (1930) The importance of symbol formation in the development of the ego, in *The Writings of Melanie Klein*, vol. 1. London: Hogarth Press, pp. 219–232.

Klein, M. (1932a) The technique of early analysis, in *The Writings of Melanie Klein*, vol. 2. London: Hogarth Press, pp. 16–34.

Klein, M. (1932b) An obsessional neurosis in a six-year-old girl, in *The Writings of Melanie Klein*, vol. 2. London: Hogarth Press, pp. 35–57.

Klein, M. (1936) Weaning, in *The Writings of Melanie Klein*, vol. 1. London: Hogarth Press, pp. 290–305.

Klein, M. (1940) Mourning and its relation to manic-depressive states, in *The Writings of Melanie Klein*, vol. 1. London: Hogarth Press, pp. 344–369.

Klein, M. (1952) On observing the behaviour of young infants, in *The Writings of Melanie Klein*, vol. 3. London: Hogarth Press, pp. 94–121.

Klein, M. (1959) Our adult world and its roots in infancy, in *The Writings of Melanie Klein*, vol. 3. London: Hogarth Press, pp. 247–263.

Rustin, M. (2022) *Finding a Way to the Child: Selected Clinical Papers 1983–2021*. London: Routledge.

Steiner, J. (ed.) (2017) *Lectures on Technique by Melanie Klein*. London: Routledge.

Strachey, J. (1934) The nature of the therapeutic action of psychoanalysis. *International Journal of Psycho-Analysis*, 50: 275–292.

Wittgenstein, L. (1929) *Culture and Value*. G. H. Von Wright and H. Nyman (eds.), P. Winch (trans.). Chicago, IL: University of Chicago Press, 1980, p. 2.

Chapter 3

Mainly the Paranoid–Schizoid Position

The Idea of Position

Klein brought together all the ideas that she had developed from her early work with children into a theory of the two positions, the "paranoid–schizoid position" and the "depressive position". She completed and laid out this overarching theory in her 1946 paper "Notes on some schizoid mechanisms". Klein had been working on the idea of position for some time before this, and had first introduced the concept in a paper on the depressive position in 1935. At that time she had not yet fully worked out her ideas on the earlier stage, the paranoid–schizoid position, that precedes the depressive position. Klein's concept of positions brought an entirely fresh way of thinking about the mind. A position is similar but significantly different from a stage; it is a state of mind with its own characteristic way of perceiving, experiencing and relating. Each position is a living, active process – it is a constellation of anxieties and the defences produced to manage them. Each position contains its own complexity of internal and external object relationships. Unlike stages, positions overlap and there is a degree of fluidity between them; progression from one position to another is not straightforward as it involves a certain amount of to-and-fro.

For Klein, the paranoid–schizoid position is the earliest and first developmental stage of the ego and is also a stage that continues to a greater or lesser extent on into childhood and adulthood. In her theory of the paranoid–schizoid position, Klein

DOI: 10.4324/9781003215714-4

brought together the following: her early ideas of loving desires on the one hand and violent hatred on the other, the theory of the life and death instincts and the early defensive activities of projection and introjection. Although Klein worked out her ideas on the depressive position first in papers written in 1935 and 1940, the paranoid–schizoid position is the ego's initial task and so I will describe it first. The main anxiety in this position is the fear of annihilation and that the good self will be overwhelmed by destructive forces; this explains Klein's use of the term paranoid. The main defence is splitting which results in a split ego, hence Klein's use of the term schizoid. Klein was influenced by, but not in complete agreement with, Ronald Fairbairn's 1944 ideas on the early defensive splitting of the ego.

Binary Splitting

Klein put forward the view that omnipotence, splitting, projection, idealization and denigration are essential defences at the start of life. She believed that, in order to survive, the infant needs to get rid of the experience of having a destructive presence inside his body. In her theory the first task of the infant is to ensure his own survival and to protect himself from being overwhelmed by the anxiety caused by this destructive presence; he achieves this by the omnipotent defensive activities of splitting and projection:

> I hold that anxiety arises from the operation of the death instinct within the organism, is felt as fear of annihilation (death) and takes the form of fear of persecution. The fear of the destructive impulse seems to attach itself at once to an object – or rather it is experienced as the fear of an uncontrollable overpowering object … The vital need to deal with anxiety forces the early ego to develop fundamental mechanisms and defences. The destructive impulse is partly projected outwards (deflection of the death instinct) and, I think, attaches itself to the first external object, the mother's breast.
>
> (Klein, 1946, p. 4)

Klein's understanding was that the infantile ego has the capacity and sophistication necessary to identify and project out its anxiety and not only this, but that it also has the capacity to separate the good feelings and experiences from the bad ones. The life instinct and loving feelings are separated from the death instinct and hating feelings, and each set of feelings along with the part of the ego in which they are experienced is projected out into the mother who is similarly separated into good and bad; the good feelings are projected into the 'good' mother/breast and the bad feelings into the 'bad' mother/breast. Some death instinct remains within and is used as aggression to defend the ego against the bad object mother/breast. Klein used the terms mother and breast interchangeably as she considered that at this early stage the infant experiences himself and those around him as unintegrated bodily parts – known as "part objects" – breast, hands, nipple, face and so on – parts that are not held together. This unintegrated state contributes to the infant's anxiety of falling apart. Klein thought that as well as providing protection, the separation of good and bad brings order.

Projective and Introjective Identification

Projective Identification

In her 1952 revised version of the 1946 paper on schizoid mechanisms, Klein referred to the process of splitting and projection as "projective identification". This term is generally attributed to Klein although there is some doubt about whether it was she who first came up with it. These mental mechanisms were attracting a great deal of interest among her immediate colleagues, for example Rosenfeld (1947) and Bion (1959), who were both patients of Klein. Even though Klein herself did not think of this concept as the most important of her ideas, projective identification is the concept that has been, and continues to be, examined and expanded more than any other. A vast body of literature has grown up detailing the part played by projective identification in emotional and cognitive development and in the relationship between analyst and patient. Projection and introjection are fundamental to all relationships, and theories about projective identification play a significant part in theories of technique, as you will see in later chapters. Klein herself, according to Gammill (1989), thought that the important task for future analysts was to better understand splitting and its relation to repression and displacement, and she is said to have referred to her 1946 paper as "my splitting paper".

Over time projective identification has become used as an umbrella term that covers different activities and therefore its use can cause confusion. For this reason, some writers have suggested subdivisions to clarify its meaning. In projective identification, the projector projects out an aspect of himself and identifies it as now residing in whoever or whatever it is projected into. This activity might be better described as 'disidentification', as it is the other, not the subject, who is identified as containing the projected aspect. Another suggested term is 'attributive' projective identification, this makes it clear that the projected aspects are attributed to someone else. Projective identification alters the subject and the object and the relationship between them. Not only is the mother treated as though she is whatever has been projected into her but also the infant experiences himself as being depleted of whatever he has projected out.

Splitting and projection – projective identification – were active in a small child who I saw for an assessment in a child psychiatry department when I was pregnant. The child had been disturbed since the birth of her sibling. Once inside my consulting room she pressed herself against the door and looked at me with frightened eyes. She pointed at me and asked, "will the baby in your tummy bite me?". I thought that she was terrified that her original wish to bite the baby in her Mummy's tummy, and by extension her wish to bite the baby in my tummy, now existed in the baby in my tummy, who she feared wanted to bite her. By means of projective identification, my child patient had become the good one and the baby in my tummy was now identified as the bad dangerous one. The result was that I had turned into a very frightening figure. This primitive way of separating good from bad can be seen all around us; it is played out in children's games with goodies and baddies and witches and devils, and of course we also see similar extreme positions in many situations. When carried out on a large

scale, splitting and projection can lead to the disastrous consequences of genocide and war. Dividing things into good and bad
is a universal and a very basic defence – "I am good, I am part of
the good group, they are bad".

Projective identification may be driven by motives other than the
straightforward wish to be rid of an unwanted part of the self; it can
be used to control the object and to avoid the painful awareness of
being separate, of being helpless or of feeling envious. Projective identification may be used to acquire someone else's skills and attributes
via 'acquisitive' projective identification – a process in which the individual gets inside (in phantasy) and takes over the other person's
attributes. This process is hard to distinguish from "introjective
identification" and Rosenfeld (1964) thought that acquisition by
projection and introjection occur simultaneously. It may be possible
to distinguish what specifically is going on from a patient's dreams
and phantasies.

Introjective Identification

The process of introjection and introjective identification is as important as projective identification. For Klein, objects are taken into the
self in different ways, ways that are dependent on the individual's stage
of life and state of mind at the time. The early objects taken in at the
start of life are imbued with omnipotence and coloured by the love
and hate – life and death instincts – that have been projected into
them. The result is that these first objects are experienced as either
extremely good or extremely bad. Klein argued that the infant needs
to feel that he has within him a powerfully good presence that is strong
enough to defend the good self against destructive bad forces. The
internalization of a good (initially ideal) stable object is in Klein's
theory essential for healthy development as it is this object that
provides the secure core around which the ego coheres.

> For I hold that the introjected good breast forms a vital part
> of the ego and exerts from the beginning a fundamental
> influence on the process of ego development and affects both
> ego structure and object relations.
>
> (Klein, 1946, p. 4)

Location and Levels of Internalization

Klein considered that the early objects are installed in both the ego and the superego and over time less extreme versions are taken in, with the result that there are layers of versions of objects within us. In a late paper (1958) Klein added the idea that the extreme early introjects are located not only in the ego and the superego but also in the deep unconscious where they remain out of touch with reality, only to be disturbed when the individual is under stress. Rosenfeld (2001) suggested that when binary splitting and projection into the object fails, the individual may project into a part of his own body, creating a "psychotic island" which can cause both hypochondria and psychosomatic illness.

Idealization and Denigration

Klein reasoned that idealization and denigration are involved in this early splitting activity and she emphasized that the initial split is extreme, between an ideal experience with an ideal mother and self on the one hand, and a terrifyingly bad mother and self on the other, which because of the extremity of its badness must be kept away at all costs. Klein (1946) wrote about a patient who she understood as wanting to annihilate this dangerous bad part of herself. The patient dreamt that

> She had to deal with a wicked girl child who was determined to murder somebody. The patient tried to influence or control the child and to extort a confession from her which would have been to the child's benefit; but she was unsuccessful. I also entered into the dream and the patient felt that I might help her in dealing with the child. Then the patient strung up the child on a tree in order to frighten her and also prevent her from doing harm. When the patient was about to pull the rope and kill the child, she woke.
>
> (Klein, 1946, p. 20)

A patient who had transitioned from male to female thirty years earlier and had lived relatively successfully as a woman, came for help when disturbed by intruding thoughts. It became clear that these thoughts came from her/his childhood memories of sexual abuse by male members of his/her family. They were the memories of the small boy she had once been, who for most of her life had been denied any conscious acknowledgement. My way of thinking about the situation was that these extremely bad experiences had been got rid of along with his male gender and his penis. For many years she/he was no longer that abused boy, that boy and his abusers no longer existed and, in the mind of this patient, they had never existed. It is possible that he may have felt that he was a devil who had been responsible for his own abuse and that he could punish the boy by eliminating him and get rid of the bad experience at the same time. But the boy with his traumatic experiences had existed and continued to live on in the patient's psyche, and for some reason the memories chose this time of his life to push their way back into consciousness – I do not know why then.

Splitting is a defensive activity that is life preserving as it protects the mind from extreme and overwhelming pain and experience, but if it is rigidly held it limits development and interferes with awareness of internal and external reality. Splitting actively structures the mind and the way in which the mind works, organizes and relates to experience. Splitting also enables us to focus on one thing and put other concerns out of our mind; we need to split in order to get on with life without being overwhelmed or in a state of confusion. We split off awareness of what is going on around us and of events far afield and this may at times cause us to feel uneasy about the people and activities that we are shutting out. It is not easy to make a judgement about what to concentrate on and what to shut out; but shutting out is essential for survival and sanity. The paradigm of the Oedipus complex in which one person is left out describes this fundamental situation and the fundamental importance and necessity of being able to bear being left out and to bear leaving others out.

As well as wanting to separate from bad experiences, there is a strong wish in all of us to hold on to good ones. It is hard to give up something that is experienced as good and even more difficult when the good thing is believed to be ideal – why would we want to lose something or someone ideal? At any one moment in the paranoid–schizoid position, the infant experiences one extreme aspect of the relationship while the other extreme aspect is denied, with the result that the paranoid–schizoid state of mind is precarious and the individual may oscillate from one extreme state to another. The ideal internal object and self are vulnerable to the inevitable reality of less-than-ideal experiences and impulses. The difficulty of keeping bad experiences and bad feelings out of awareness means that sudden reversals threaten and often do occur.

As you can see, splitting is not only between good and bad – there is also a split between what is conscious and what unconscious. Close to the beginning of her analysis, a patient who talked to me as though I were ideal and gave me compliments, was shocked to hear herself say, "I am sure what you say will be useless". This was not what she had planned – she was in the middle of saying something very positive; this denigrated but denied view of what I had to offer was closer to the surface than she had realized. Keeping the reality of one's own negative feelings and ideas out of sight and out of consciousness involves continuous activity as does keeping out all information that disproves the 'facts' that one wants to maintain. Totalitarian states keep control of the media to ensure that only one version of reality is available to their population. Dictatorships operate in a paranoid–schizoid manner and regularly use violent means to maintain their own version of events and to suppress alternative views.

Omnipotence

All this defensive activity in the infant is achieved omnipotently; in an omnipotent state of mind, phantasy is reality. Klein's infant, like Freud's, hallucinates the breast. For Klein, the infant sucking his thumb believes that he possesses or actually *is* the breast. This phantasy to some extent protects him from feelings of hunger, helplessness and frustration. An individual in an omnipotent state of mind believes that he has the power to separate the good and bad aspects of himself and others, that he has the power to place his feelings and experiences outside himself into someone else and that he has the power to eliminate some experiences completely. Reality is under his control and is whatever he phantasizes it to be. Others are treated as though they are whatever has been projected into them.

A paper by David Bell (2015) provides an example of omnipotence. An adolescent in treatment insisted that he keep the door of his consulting room open during her sessions. After a period of treatment Bell thought it would be possible to close the door and told her that he was going to do this. She replied "I can do what I want, when I want". He closed the door and heard the girl whisper to herself: "the door is open". The next day she came into the room and as he raised himself to shut the door, she shouted: "Go and shut the door shit-head". Bell understood her words to herself "the door is open" to be a desperate attempt to manage the threat to her omnipotence, rather than a complete delusion. The second defensive manoeuvre in which he was denigrated was in his view linked to a manic excitement about being in control. The excitement of omnipotence, of having power, adds an additional layer of interference against the development of the capacity to recognize reality.

It is not easy to disprove the beliefs of someone in an omnipotent state of mind. One four-year-old child complained to her mother that a framed collage of photos contained more photos of her baby brother than of her. The mother carefully counted the photos with her, there were two of each of the children and one of them both; the number of photos of each child was equal. "No", answered the child, "there is one more of him". Her mother replied sympathetically and counted again "look that's not right, there are two of each of you". The child continued to insist, "There are three of him", and added, "but the extra one is invisible". While it is hard to tackle the invisible, knowing that there is something in another person's mind that is invisible to us is an important start, and even better if we know what it is. The analyst's job is to find out what exists in the mind of her patient, get it out into the open, talk about it and hope that the patient becomes able to recognize what exists in the mind rather than in the external world and becomes able to differentiate their internal reality from the external.

Splitting along Other Planes

Awareness of the Split

Individuals attempting to operate a totalitarian state of mind, being both the controller of the media and on the receiving end of the distorted information, may be aware of what they are up to. This may be revealed in dreams or associations. Two patients of mine actively dismissed my comments while denying that they did this. I could see that at one level each had an awareness of what she was doing; one told me of a dream in which there was a small girl in her house who was engaged in throwing food out of the fridge and the other patient complained that there was someone who kept moving the fresh food to the back of the fridge where it was unnoticed and so was unfit to eat by the time it was found. Another patient told me that all the time that he was maintaining a negative version of me, he had an uneasy sense inside that what he was saying was not quite right. Bion (1957) wrote that in the psychotic patient there exists a non-psychotic part of the personality that is aware of reality, an awareness that Freud had written about many years earlier, describing how even in severe cases

> there was a normal person hidden, who, like a detached spectator, watched the hub-hub of illness go past him … what occurs in all these cases is a psychical *split*. Two psychical attitudes have been formed instead of a single one: one, the normal one, which takes account of reality, and another which under the influence of the instincts detaches the ego from reality.
>
> (Freud, 1939, p. 202)

Other Planes

Splits can be between taking account of reality and ignoring it and splits can also be between emotion and thought or between the mind and the body. One patient who came for help did so because she cried but did not know why. Another patient came to see me because his family wanted him to do something about the way in which he was cut off from his feelings. I learnt that he was dominated by what he called the 'real' him who he differentiated from the bodily him. He was, for example, terrified of heights and told me that he took himself to the edge of cliffs but that he was completely safe because the bodily him was not the real him; he was safe with the real him, the real him always looked after him. Here the split was between a powerful omnipotent part of the personality that he referred to as the real him, and a vulnerable bodily part more in touch with physical and emotional reality that was the one that I thought of as the real him. This kind of organization of the personality, now commonly referred to as a pathological organization will be discussed in more detail in a later chapter. As time went on, I learnt more about the way in which my patient was excited by having power over a vulnerable feeling part of himself and excited by torturing that part. Dictators also may become excited by their own power and excited by the experience of locating powerlessness and pain in others and torturing it there.

Fragmentary Splitting and Psychosis

Klein's infant starts off in an unintegrated state. He gradually becomes held together by the natural process of maturity as well as by the process of taking in a good object around which his ego begins to cohere. All being well, over time and with repeated good experiences the infant achieves the binary split of the paranoid–schizoid position. If he is well cared for by someone who understands and responds to his needs; if he is attended to in a loving thoughtful way, fed when he is hungry and held when he is anxious, he will take in these good experiences, he will become stronger and he will build up a sense of having something good inside. This good internal object will provide a sense of security and will strengthen the infant's capacity to bear the difficult experiences of being hungry, anxious, helpless, and having to wait, and he will begin the depressive position process of integrating these bad experiences and the bad feelings that accompany them into a more whole sense of himself.

In some cases, though, the infant will not become sufficiently gathered-together to start to integrate the different aspects of the world or himself and, rather than being reduced, splits will become increasingly extreme and rigidly held. Extreme states of mind, denial of reality, omnipotent thinking, idealization and denigration are seen in mentally and emotionally disturbed people and in psychiatric patients; Klein concluded that such individuals have not moved beyond the early primitive defences of the paranoid–schizoid position.

Other infants fail to achieve a binary split or only have a very fragile sense of a good internal object; these infants are vulnerable to fragmentation:

> The infant's feeling of having inside a good and complete breast may, however, be shaken by frustration and anxiety. As a result, the division between the good and bad breast may be difficult to maintain and the infant may feel that the good breast too is in bits.
>
> (Klein, 1946, p. 5)

It is possible to recognize an everyday state of falling apart in children when faced with tasks that feel too difficult. This is a state that we may recognize in ourselves when we are confronted with something that we cannot understand or cannot do. We can start to feel very anxious, very angry, unable to think and tormented by the suggestion that we should do the impossible thing that is being demanded of us; we may feel in danger of going completely to pieces. Normally this state of mind is transitory and occurs when we are under stress, but for some, a fragmentary state remains a constant threat.

When bad experiences predominate, the individual may repeatedly resort to fragmentation. For bad experiences that threaten to overwhelm, the only defence may be to fragment the mind and break the bad experience into small pieces. Klein's daughter, Schmideberg, thought that fragmentation reduces the power of the bad experience. Klein agreed and wrote "the ego in varying degrees fragments itself and its objects, and in this way achieves a dispersal of the destructive impulses and of internal persecutory anxieties" (Klein, 1957, p. 191). A fragmented individual is weakened and no longer has the mental capacity that is needed to piece things together and make sense of his experience. Some individuals whose lives are dominated by bad experiences may repeatedly resort to fragmentation. The idea of fragmentary splitting was taken up by Rosenfeld (1950) who wrote about psychotic states and the desperate confusion experienced by fragmented individuals, and by Bion (1959) who brought attention to the sense of an internal bad object that attacks the capacity to perceive and to make links. Klein wrote about schizophrenics as follows:

> Another factor which contributes to the loneliness of the schizophrenic is confusion. This is the result of a number of factors, particularly the fragmentation of the ego and the excessive use of projective identification, so that he constantly feels himself not only to be in bits, but to be mixed up with other people. He is then unable to distinguish between the good and bad parts of the self, between the good and the bad object and between external and internal reality. The schizophrenic thus, cannot understand himself or trust himself. These factors allied with his paranoid distrust of others, result in a state of withdrawal which destroys his ability to make object relations and to gain from them the reassurance and pleasure which can counteract loneliness by strengthening the ego.
>
> (Klein, 1963, p. 304)

Some disturbed individuals construct a self from the fragments and hold themselves together by means of a delusion. In her 1946 paper Klein uses Freud's example of the case of Schreber as an illustration of someone whose internal and external worlds are catastrophically fragmented and whose defence against the resulting confusion is to live in a state of delusion.

An Earlier Unintegrated State

A number of writers have put forward the idea of the existence of a pre-paranoid–schizoid state of unintegration during which the infant needs an outside agent that holds him together; this can be a holding mother (Winnicott) or a containing mother (Bion). The absence of an object providing this essential function grossly impedes emotional and cognitive development, causes early physical and mental experiences to remain confused together and this can result in psychosomatic illness or in the individual using his body in to hold himself together mentally (Bick, 1968; Bion, 1962; Winnicott, 1949). The debate about this earlier stage continues (Waddell, 2006).

Psychoanalysis with Psychotic Patients

Klein's ideas brought optimism to colleagues who were at that time working with psychotic patients, in particular Bion, Rosenfeld and Hanna Segal, another of Klein's patients and an important contributor to the understanding of Klein's ideas; but sadly psychotic states of mind have not been found easy to change. Nonetheless Klein's ideas have proved enormously useful in understanding these patients. To give one example, Leslie Sohn, drawing on his work with ten highly disturbed patients in forensic settings, wrote a paper based mainly on three of them who had attacked strangers in public places. One patient, for example, had assaulted a stranger on a platform of a London underground station and attempted to push him off on to the line. Sohn argued that the patients, each in their own way, managed upsetting and disturbing events by inhabiting a delusional world, and that it was when this way of managing failed and reality intruded and spoilt the delusional world, that the patient resorted to a more violent and concrete way of getting rid of upsetting feelings.

Two of the assaults took place after the patients had suffered a loss that could not be managed in their usual delusional way. One patient had been told that he had lost his job, another had lost the sense of having a good object. Two of the patients seemed to believe that they could then push their unmanageable feelings of loss into their victims via the attack, and in doing so change places with their victim – taking for themselves their victim's life. Sohn observed that the victims were chosen because they were seen as being in a good state; one was a tourist who looked happy, and two victims were described as, "totally free of any sign of misery". The intolerable loss of something good was relocated into the stranger who lost his safe place in the world. The third patient projected his suicidal feelings into his victim and then attacked him in order to frighten him out of it.

The Danger of Omnipotence in the Analyst

Klein's ideas provide a warning for all who work in the helping professions and who long to be a powerful healing force for the good. This is a dangerous longing and particularly so when combined with the patient's infantile longing for an ideal saviour who will cure him – a longing that is aroused by the treatment situation. This issue is the topic of Tom Main's (1957) paper "The ailment" in which he documented the antitherapeutic action of this dynamic in the Cassell, a hospital that provides psychoanalytically informed treatment along therapeutic community lines. Main detailed the way in which a staff member's wish to be ideally helpful to her patient, when paired with the patient's desire for an ideal carer, provoked each staff member's omnipotence and convinced them that they could provide the perfect experience for their patient. The staff member inevitably failed to be everything that her patient wanted, and when the patient came up against the limits of what the staff member could realistically offer, he responded with anger and moved away into a relationship with a newly idealized member of staff, leaving the previously idealized, but now denigrated, staff member demoralized and depressed by her failure. In this destructive dynamic, the patient failed to address his own problems. The conclusion drawn from the paper is that infantile longings and the rage stirred up by their frustration exist in both staff and patients, and if not contained will cause splitting in the staff group, which will in turn drastically hinder patients' ability to integrate the splits in their own psyches. Staff members need to be helped to know about and bear the limits of what they have to offer. The reality of what can and cannot be achieved has to be faced by clinicians and patients alike. Not an easy task, but the task of the depressive position which is the subject of the next chapter.

Primitive Defences and the Social and Political

Just as Klein took an interest in the effect of the threatening political situation of World War II on the internal world of her patients, particularly fears of destruction from within, so Segal and a number of analysts from different theoretical backgrounds took a passionate interest in the effect of the threat of nuclear war. In one of her several papers on this subject, Segal quotes Glover (1933):

> The first promise of the atomic age is that it can make some of our nightmares come true. The capacity so painfully acquired by normal man to distinguish between sleep, hallucination, delusion and the objective reality of wakened life has for the first time in history been seriously weakened.
>
> (quoted in Segal, 1987)

Segal (1987) argued that the existence of nuclear weapons with their threat of total annihilation mobilizes the primitive omnipotent defences of splitting, projection and denial to an even greater extent than does conventional warfare. This theme of denial and disavowal of our destructiveness has been taken up by many analysts and members of other disciplines writing on the subject of climate change denial and in particular by Sally Weintrobe (2013).

Fahkry Davids (2011, 2020), addressing issues on racism, has attended not only to the way in which the mechanisms of splitting and projection are used by individuals and groups to place unwanted characteristics into members of another group while claiming 'good' attributes for themselves, but also to the way in which these processes interact with, are influenced by, and are supported by wider social forces.

References

Bell, D. (2015) The death drive: Phenomenological perspectives in contemporary Kleinian theory. *International Journal of Psycho-Analysis*, 96: 411–423.

Bick, E. (1968) The experience of the skin in early object relations. *International Journal of Psycho-Analysis*, 49: 484–486.

Bion, W. (1957) Differentiation of the psychotic from the non-psychotic personalities. *International Journal of Psycho-Analysis*, 38: 266–275.

Bion, W. (1959) Attacks on linking. *International Journal of Psycho-Analysis*, 40: 308–315.

Bion, W. (1962) A theory of thinking. *International Journal of Psychoanalysis*, 43: 306-310

Davids, M. F. (2011) *Internal Racism: A Psychoanalytic Approach to Race and Difference.* Basingstoke: Palgrave MacMillan.

Davids, M. F. (2020) Psychoanalysis and black lives. *International Journal of Psycho-Analysis*, 101: 1039–1047.

Fairbairn, R. (1944) Endopsychic structure considered in terms of object-relationships. *International Journal of Psycho-Analysis*, 25: 70–92.

Freud, S. (1939) The psychical apparatus and the external world, *S.E.* 23, p. 202).

Gammill, J. (1989) Some personal reflections on Melanie Klein. *Melanie Klein and Object Relations*, 7(2).

Klein, M. (1935) A contribution to the psychogenesis of manic-depressive states, in *The Writings of Melanie Klein*, vol. 1. London: Hogarth Press, pp. 236–289.

Klein M. (1940) Mourning and its relation to manic-depressive states, in *The Writings of Melanie Klein*, vol. 1. London: Hogarth Press, pp. 344–369.

Klein, M. (1946) Notes on some schizoid mechanisms, in *The Writings of Melanie Klein*, vol. 3. London: Hogarth Press, pp. 1–24.

Klein, M. (1957) Envy and gratitude, in *The Writings of Melanie Klein*, Vol. 3. London: Hogarth Press, pp. 176–235.

Klein, M. (1958) On the development of mental functioning, in *The Writings of Melanie Klein*, vol. 3. London: Hogarth Press, pp. 236–246.

Klein, M. (1963) On the sense of loneliness, in *The Writings of Melanie Klein*, Vol. 3. London: Hogarth Press, pp. 300–313.

Main, T. (1957) The ailment. *British Journal of Medical Psychology*, 30:3, 129–1454.

Rosenfeld, H. (1947) Analysis of a schizophrenic state with depersonalization. *International Journal of Psycho-analysis*, 28: 130–139.

Rosenfeld, H. (1950) Notes on the psychopathology of confusional states in chronic schizophrenia. *International Journal of Psycho-analysis*, 31d: 132–137.

Rosenfeld, H. (1964) On the psychopathology of narcissism: A clinical approach. *International Journal of Psycho-analysis*, 45: 332–337.

Rosenfeld, H. (2001) The relationship between psychosomatic symptoms and latent psychotic states, in F. de Masi (ed.), *Herbert Rosenfeld at work: The Italian Seminars.* London: Karnac, pp. 24–44.

Segal, H. (1972) A delusional system as a defence against the re-emergence of a catastrophic situation. *International Journal of Psycho-analysis*, 53: 393–401.

Segal, H. (1987) Silence is the real crime. *International Review of Psychoanalysis*, 14: 3–12.

Sohn, L. (1995) Unprovoked assaults—Making sense of apparently random violence. *International Review of Psychoanalysis*, 76: 565–575.

Steiner, J. (1981) Perverse relationships between parts of the self: A clinical illustration. *International Journal of Psychoanalysis*, 63: 241–251.

Waddell, M. (2006) Integration, unintegration, disintegration: An introduction. *Journal of Child Psychotherapy*, 32: 148–152.

Weintrobe, S. (ed.) (2013) *Engaging with Climate Change: Psychoanalytic and Interdisciplinary Perspectives*. London: Routledge.

Winnicott, D.W. (1949) Mind and its relation to the psyche-soma, in *Through Paediatrics to Psycho-analysis*. London: Hogarth (1982), pp. 243–254.

Chapter 4

Mainly the Depressive Position

As I have described in the previous chapter, the first task of the infant in the paranoid–schizoid position is to separate good experiences and feelings from bad. The next task of the ego, and the task of the depressive position, is to bring these two strands of experience together. This is a difficult and complex task full of losses; it involves taking back projections and fitting unwanted aspects together with the acceptable and wanted aspects. Taking back projections and taking responsibility for ourselves involves being able to be separate.

A patient's dream, brought towards the end of her analysis, showed an understanding of the task. My patient started the session by telling me that her daughter had asked if she could use her car; to do so her daughter would have to drive on my patient's insurance. Here is the dream:

> There was an estuary which went into the sea and as it went inland along its left-hand side were a series of harbours which had jetties into the estuary and in all the harbours on the jetties there were canoes which were made of polystyrene. I was walking along the side of the estuary on a concrete walkway, and I had a polystyrene canoe which I had got earlier from an inland harbour. As I got close to the estuary there was a man in one of these harbours and I asked him about the paddle. I was worried about the paddle and I asked, "does the canoe work with one paddle or do you need two?" He replied "one paddle". I also asked about the battery which I had in my other hand. It

DOI: 10.4324/9781003215714-5

was a sort of black box, and it was heavy and I asked him how it went into the canoe. He told me it fitted into the back of the canoe, and this made me think to myself that therefore the canoe must have a motor. I asked how it worked. I was frightened of going by myself and frightened because I saw that the sea was a bit choppy out in the estuary and I saw white horses – white spray on the top of waves.

Here there are two separated objects that need to be fitted together – a very light white canoe and a heavy black box. The patient had various associations to her dream; her first thought was that the black box made her think of mourning and sadness, and her later thought was that the black box of an airplane contains the flight information that is examined after a crash.

I think the dream illustrates my patient's fear of the approaching end of her analysis and her anxieties about having to do things on her own without me; of paddling her own canoe and no longer driving on my insurance – no longer having me available to be responsible for her and to carry the knowledge and anxieties that she did not want. The black box in the dream shows her awareness of needing to understand how and why things go wrong and to know also about the part she plays. I think she realized that her buoyancy had depended on keeping away from knowledge and experience of the difficulties and the downside of things, but she now felt that this would not help her in the choppy seas of her future life. She needed this knowledge, knowledge about aspects of herself that she did not like – her aggression for example – as it would help her to negotiate life without me. But knowing about our own aggression brings heaviness – it brings the pain and anxiety of guilt.

In Klein's theory of the depressive position the different aspects of the self and other, split into good and bad, are brought into contact with one another. The developing infant becomes aware that the mother who feeds and comforts him, who provides good experiences – the mother who he loves – is not always good, she is also the one who is responsible for bad experiences, she does not feed or comfort him whenever he is in need, she is the person who leaves him and who he hates for not being there when he wants. In fact, she is the one who at times he will want to harm or even murder.

Klein reasoned that an infant who has repeated good experiences of a mother who returns and who gives food and comfort will take these experiences inside himself where they will build up a sense of stable goodness. This good internal object will reduce the severity of bad experiences. Klein thought that the infant manages frustration with the omnipotent defence of hallucination. So for example, a hungry baby whose mother is absent sucks his thumb and believes that his good mother is present or that he is his own good mother. With the arrival of the real mother, the hallucinated good object is replaced by an actual good experience and this leads to some kind of rudimentary memory of a good experience. The infant will be to some extent sustained by this memory during the next absence. Depending on the length of the absence and the degree of frustration he may also once again have to depend on a hallucinated object. Gradually the infant builds up a sense of good object that is absent but returns. As you can see, this idea also introduces the concept of time, the present does not go on for ever. We lose the ever-present good experience but we are strengthened by the knowledge that the current bad experience is likely to end.

Mourning and the Many Losses of the Depressive Position

Mourning is central to the depressive position. The depressive position involves the acceptance of the loss of what we do not have and what we cannot control. The mourning involved in accepting these losses is fundamental to the developmental process of the depressive position. An infant or any of us beginning to integrate unwanted aspects of ourselves and our objects will become aware that neither we nor our objects are as good as we might wish. We must give up and mourn an ideal version of ourselves and our objects, and give up the idea that we are part of a perfect loving relationship. Omnipotence, omniscience, total possession, idealization of the self and other – all must be given up. The individual must face the reality that he is a limited and separate being and that his loved ones have lives of their own. It is important to note that links exist between the depressive position and the Oedipus complex. Both involve the loss of the ideal relationship, the loss of a relationship in which you are number one and in which you possess your mother or father.

> The sorrow and concern about the feared loss of the 'good' objects, that is to say, the depressive position, is, in my experience, the deepest source of the painful conflicts in the Oedipus situation.
>
> (Klein, 1940, p. 345)

The infant in the depressive position must recognize that he neither possesses nor controls his mother; she is not his, she is not always there with him. At times she is somewhere else with someone else; she has other relationships. It is not easy for any of us to face that we are not the only or the most important person; it is not easy to bear the horrible feelings of being left out of an important relationship and to feel jealous, small and unwanted. Working through the depressive position involves working through the Oedipus complex and vice versa. There is also an inverted Oedipus complex. Klein, like Freud, considered bisexuality to be inherent and she argued that in each of us there is an inverted Oedipus complex in which we desire the parent of the same sex and are full of jealousy and hatred towards the parent of the opposite sex; the positive and inverted Oedipus complexes oscillate and both must be worked through.

> Each object, therefore, is in turn liable to become at times good, at times bad. This movement to-and-fro between various aspects of the primary imagos implies a close interaction between the early stages of the inverted and positive Oedipus complex.
>
> (Klein, 1945, p. 409)

Ultimately the two parents are seen as a couple, the sense of a strong loving caring couple is of immense benefit, promotes development and enables the individual himself to be part of a creative couple.

Klein also considered the early working through in part object terms. She reasoned that the 'good' breast provides the secure base from which the infant can turn his desire outward onto another 'good' object, the penis. This turning away is driven in part by love for the good breast and in part by the frustration that is felt towards the 'bad' breast. The penis also frustrates and so the infant oscillates between the two part objects, introjecting both good and bad aspects of each and gradually bringing the part objects together into a whole object.

The experience of being separate is frightening, if you are on your own you must rely on your own capacities and if you are a helpless infant, you are completely dependent on someone else to take care of you. Many individuals have a great deal of difficulty in being separate and may want, or believe that they need, someone else who is present all the time and who they can call on whenever they feel the need, someone over whom they have control. This someone would also take responsibility and relieve them of guilt – like my patient's daughter, they want to drive on someone else's insurance.

As extreme states of mind reduce, and as we become increasingly realistic in our perception of ourselves and the world around us, we face a sense of the limits of our own power. This awareness can be depressing but it is also a great relief not to be responsible for everything. However, if we or no other being is all powerful and all knowing, we have no certainty about what is good and what is bad. The loss of this certainty brings with it the anxiety and uncertainty about what or who is good or bad, about who can be trusted, and importantly raises the question of whether the powers of badness are more powerful than those of goodness, whether the feelings of hatred, rage, violence, jealousy and envy are stronger than the feelings of love and gratitude and concern. The infant and all of us, again and again, must find out from experience. Many troubled and traumatized individuals would rather hang on to certainty, even if it is the certainty of a bad world, than endure the experience of uncertainty and having to use their own experience and their own minds to work things out. All of us to some extent prefer the certainty of what we know and resist having our beliefs disrupted.

Klein considered that our ability to mourn losses in later life is dependent on our having negotiated our early losses. Freud argued that if we are to separate from someone whom we love, give them up and bear the loss we need to take that loved person into ourselves and identify with them, they become a part of us. In a paper on mourning, Britton has written about the importance of our giving psychic life to our lost objects so that they have a life beyond their own material transient existence; the process of mourning is invaluable as it provides us with the good internal objects that sustain us. In his 2018 paper he quotes Rilke:

> How we squander our hours of pain.
> How we gaze beyond them into the bitter duration
> To see if they have an end. Though they are really
> Our winter-enduing foliage, our dark evergreen,
> One season in our inner year – not only a season
> In time – but a place and settlement, foundation and soil and home.
>
> (Rilke, 1969, cited in Britton, 2018, p. 205)

Both Freud and Klein were aware of the enormous difficulty that their patients had in separating from someone they loved, and both understood that mourning is a difficult and painstaking task in which aspects of the lost loved one are given up piece by piece.

> Each single one of the memories and expectations in which the libido is bound to the object is brought up and hypercathected, and detachment of the libido is accomplished in respect of it. Why this compromise by which the command of reality is carried out piecemeal should be so extraordinarily painful is not at all easy to explain in terms of economics.
>
> (Freud 1917, p. 245)

The Interference of Hostility in the Mourning Process and the Importance of Loving Feelings

Freud placed importance on the fact that hostility towards the loved lost object interferes with mourning (1917) and I go into this in greater detail in the next chapter when considering the superego and its destructive potential. Klein (1940) gave a clear example from her own experience when writing about the difficulties faced by Mrs A, who was Klein herself. She explained how the obstacles that she initially encountered in mourning the death of her son were due to the complexity of the feelings of hostility and rivalry that she felt towards her brother and her mother. Hostility towards the original object, her mother, affected subsequent mourning. At first Klein denied her son's death and felt no pain, but then she had a dream.

> *She saw two people, a mother and son, the mother was wearing a black dress. The dreamer knew that this boy had died, or was going to die. No sorrow entered into her feelings, but there was a trace of hostility towards the two people.*
>
> (Klein, 1940, p. 356)

Using this and other dreams and thoughts, Klein recognized that she was unconsciously asserting that it was her brother, a rival – her mother's son – who had died and not her son. She realized that she had felt a degree of triumph over her brother and over her mother too, also a rival, for having lost a son. Klein's triumphant feelings caused her pangs of guilt. By acknowledging her hostility and the accompanying guilt, Klein recovered compassion for her mother and in turn compassion for herself, and she was then able to face and bear her own loss. Like the infants whom she wrote about, Klein felt pangs of guilt and remorse for having had destructive wishes towards her mother, the very person who she had loved and most depended on and who she needed now as a good sustaining object inside herself to help her bear the pain of her son's death. Just as children need a good internal mother to support them, so too Klein needed to recover the sense that she had an internal supportive mother; a mother who had not been destroyed by her feelings of hate and rivalry.

Depressive Guilt

Klein had the view that as the infant becomes aware of his feelings of hatred, he fears that he has damaged his loved object and this causes great feelings of regret, remorse, anxiety and guilt – in Klein's terms 'depressive anxiety' and 'depressive guilt'. It is very painful to realize that you have hated or do hate and may have injured someone who you love. Klein thought that during this period loving feelings are in the ascendency and this helps the infant to bear the guilt that he feels about the wrongs that he has done, his crossness, unkindness and violent thoughts and actions.

> All the enjoyments which the baby lives through in relation to his mother are so many proofs to him that the loved object *inside as well as outside* is not injured, is not turned into a vengeful person. The increase of love and trust, and the diminishing of fears through happy experiences, help the baby step by step to overcome his depression and feeling of loss (mourning).
>
> (Klein, 1940, pp. 346–347)

The Importance of the Environment

As you can see from the quote above, Klein believed that the environment plays an important part in emotional development, a point that is often overlooked by her critics. Here is a more detailed example

> External experiences are, of course, of great importance in these developments. For instance, in the case of a patient who showed depressive and schizoid features, the analysis brought up with great vividness his early experiences in babyhood, to such an extent that in some sessions physical sensations in the throat or digestive organs occurred. The patient had been weaned suddenly at four months of age because his mother fell ill. In addition, he did not see his mother for four weeks. When she returned, she found the child greatly changed. He had been a lively baby, interested in his surroundings and he seemed to have lost this interest. He had become apathetic. He had accepted the substitute food fairly easily and in fact never refused food. But he did not thrive on it any more, lost weight and had a good deal of digestive trouble.
>
> (Klein, 1946, p. 15)

A damaged or angry mother will confirm the infant's anxieties rather than disprove them. The state of the mother, or caretaker, is of great importance. An angry infant in a state of omnipotence with an angry or sick or depressed mother will fear his own destructiveness and will feel that his fears are confirmed and that he has made the mother ill. Similarly, an adult who is unsure about his own destructiveness who has a depressed partner might feel that his love and liveliness are no good and at worse that he is destructive; he might as a result become withdrawn and lifeless. A child with a violent parent may feel that it is his violence that has caused the parent to be violent.

The state of the parent makes a difference to the experience of the infant or child. But if the parent is well enough and loving enough, then the child encounters a reality that is safe, a reality that is not destroyed by his rage; then he learns the difference between what is in his mind and what is external – he learns from experience. The sense of a parent in a good state, a parent who is cared for and supported, the sense of a strong parental couple provides security. Similarly, a patient who feels that his analyst herself has the security of other significant relationships will feel safely held. The patient who feels emotionally held and understood by his analyst and whose constitution contains a balance of love and hate will feel secure enough to allow himself to know about unhappy experiences and hateful or even murderous feelings that earlier had been split off from their loving feelings. He will be able to mourn the loss of himself as a perfectly loving person and as the extremes reduce, he will become increasingly realistic in his knowledge of himself and his perception of the world around him. He will be able to express his gratitude for the love and care that he has received and express his sorrow for any upset or hurt that he has caused.

Klein's mother will have suffered from the death of two of her children but the love that Klein had for her mother and felt from her in return enabled her to face her rivalrous feelings, experience concern and guilt about them, and feel her mother's concern for her. Klein was able to separate from her mother, she was not her mother, her son was not her mother's son, she could not save her mother from pain, she could only feel sorrow and concern for her.

The Pain of Guilt and the Drive for Reparation

Freud wrote about the "part played by love in the origin of conscience and the fatal inevitability of the sense of guilt" (Freud, 1930a, p. 132) and, in the words of O'Shaughnessy, "This is where Freud took us and left us" (2018). Our primitive urges and hostile phantasies towards our primary objects leave us having to manage feelings of guilt. Our happiness or sadness depends on the state of our internal objects and our sense of how they are. In Klein's theory of the depressive position she introduced a new idea, the idea that the loving concern of depressive guilt will drive a wish to make things better – to make reparation. This concept of reparation lies at the heart of the depressive position and the capacity to make things better is of enormous significance to us all. As we move from a paranoid–schizoid state of mind into a depressive state of mind our concern changes from being anxious about our own survival to concern about the survival of those who we love and care about. Our love and concern for those who have cared for us brings us happiness, this strengthens our sense of having something good inside and this in turn helps us to be creative and give something good back. Very early on in her work with children Klein recognized the extent of their anxieties about the state of their objects.

> we might see the mother cooked and eaten and the two brothers dividing the meal between them ... But such a manifestation of primitive tendencies is invariably followed by anxiety and by performances which show how the child now tries to make good and to atone for that which he has done.
>
> (Klein, 1927, p. 175)

However, it is not that easy to make things better, we have limited power and resources, and it can be beyond our capacity to put things right. Repair is usually a very slow and incomplete process during which we must tolerate knowing about the damage that we have caused, we must endure feelings of guilt and sadness at our object's sadness, we must bear knowing that we are not as good or as powerful as we might wish – it goes on. If we can tolerate all of these 'depressive anxieties' and 'depressive guilt', that is the depression of containing damaged objects, we will be able to move forward and can try to make things better while facing the pain of the limits of what we can do. Klein described how a child might feel in the following words.

> there is anxiety how to put the bits together in the right way and at the right time; how to pick out the good bits and do away with the bad ones; how to bring the object to life when it has been put together; and there is the anxiety of being interfered with in this task by bad objects and by one's own hatred, etc.
>
> (Klein, 1935, p. 269)

If the individual finds himself in a situation where he must face a considerable amount of damage, the feelings of guilt may too strong – Klein's term for this is persecutory guilt. Persecutory guilt may cause the individual to retreat from the depressive position and to fall back into paranoid–schizoid ways of managing. An extreme example is of an inpatient in a psychiatric unit who was persecuted by the guilt of his incestuous relationship with his daughter. He desperately asked the doctors to remove a part of his brain that contained his awareness of what he had done and he compulsively washed his genitals with bleach; an action that was both a desperate attempt to cleanse the offending part of himself and also a horrible method of punishment. Others go to less extreme lengths; for example, they may deny that there is anything wrong or may acknowledge that there is something wrong but argue that they are in no way responsible for the damage; or, if they do accept some responsibility, they come up with reasons to justify the actions that they took and so exonerate themselves from guilt.

Manic and Obsessional Reparation

Some individuals recognize the damage but cling to the belief that they have the capacity to make it better, and ideally make it better quickly. These individuals come up with a quick solution in which guilt is only suffered for a short time. Reparative action based on this kind of omnipotent belief is known as 'manic reparation'. Manic reparation fails to address the problem, and in the end it makes the situation worse. It is important to recognize, though, that manic reparation does contain some positive motivation. Manic solutions play a part in normal development. Small children do not have the resources to make things better and so they turn to magical solutions. I am sure that you will be able to think of examples of the way in which children draw on imaginary magical powers to make things better, wave a magic wand, become superman, tell you that you are well now. It can be very touching to have a child want to make you better with pretend medicine. It is less touching and can make things worse if an adult tries to force a quick cure onto you, refuses to acknowledge the damage that has been done and demands that you agree that everything is alright now. A significant aspect of this kind of behaviour is that the manic person is in control, has a sense of his own power and can enjoy a sense of triumph. The manic individual does not take the other person into consideration, does not necessarily give the others what they want or need; he gives what he wants to give. The activity is more about the manic individual, how he feels and how he is seen, than about the true feelings of others. This activity is not about genuine concern and taking care of the other.

'Obsessional reparation' also involves omnipotence. The obsessional character feels that he must repair things perfectly as only perfection will satisfy. The obsessional individual must be in complete control. Obsessional reparation involves close attention to detail in contrast to manic reparation which can be carried out in sweeping gestures. Obsessional repair is never complete and has to be done over and over again. As the ideal but persecuting figure who demands repair is not satisfied by anything less than perfection, all attempts at repair are doomed to fail. The obsessional can become caught up in increasingly desperate behaviour and drive himself and other people mad. Both manic and obsessional individuals are identified with a powerful object who has the capacity to repair and are bound up with and persecuted by the damaged objects who they feel they must repair. Such individuals live in a concrete world – phantasy is not differentiated from reality.

Both manic and obsessional individuals need to do it all themselves as a repair is not felt to be perfect if they have needed help; anyone who needs help is inferior. But we all need help. It is easy to see this with children who of course need help. Klein wrote movingly about the distress felt by some of her child patients when they had broken their toys and needed her to help them mend things and to clear up the mess that they had made. If you want to make things better you may well need help from others and if you have hurt someone you do rely on their generosity in accepting your apology.

Reparation and Creativity

Klein linked the urge to create to the idea of reparation, to the wish to restore and repair the injured object. Others have suggested that the striving for perfection in a work of art involves a wish to restore the parents. Segal argued that true art is a depressive act; it provides a medium in which destructive and constructive emotions can be resolved. Segal contrasted "chocolate box" images with what she considered to be art – in the latter ugliness is depicted with beauty (1974). In a similar vein Britton (1998) contrasted "truth seeking and truth evading fiction"; truth evading fiction being escapist and based on wish-fulfilling daydream and psychic illusion, as opposed to truth seeking fiction which provides a true representation of psychic reality.

Symbolization

Letting Go of Omnipotence and the Move from the Concrete to the Symbolic

In less extreme cases where the persecution can be borne, the patient needs to be helped to bear knowing about the 'crimes', that cannot be cleansed away. He has also to separate from objects that he cannot repair and make a place for them in his mind. This involves bearing the anxiety, guilt and sorrow at the damage that his objects have suffered and facing the limits of what can be repaired. This may also include an appreciation of the limits of his power to damage. He may recognize that the damage is not his responsibility alone and that repair is not solely his responsibility either. Letting go of omnipotence releases him from the torture of having to repair his object.

Klein described the way in which she needed to separate from her dead son if she was to be able to continue on in life herself.

> She was flying with her son, and he disappeared. She felt that this meant his death – that he was drowned. She felt as if she, too, were to be drowned – but then she made an effort and drew away from the danger, back to life.

(Klein, 1940, p. 358)

Identification with the loved dead one is a way of keeping that person alive; some individuals will live in a half dead way themselves rather than separate from their dead objects. One highly unusual but vivid example is of a paralyzed child who I was asked to see in the children's ward of a hospital. The doctors had been unable to find any physiological cause for her paralysis. In speaking to her parents, I learnt that the child's grandmother had recently died in another country. The family had decided not to let the girl know about the death, as the child and her grandmother had been extremely close. The parents told me that the grandmother had been paralyzed for some years prior to her death. I suggested to them that the child knew about the death of her grandmother and that they talk to her about it; they did – the paralysis disappeared. I have only ever met one case like this, but I think it illustrates a concrete identification with a lost object as a defence against mourning.

The development of the ability to symbolize is part of the depressive process. We need to separate from our objects in the material world and place them in the form of symbols in our minds. But some traumatic experiences evade the process of symbolization and then the process that Ignes Sodre calls "ordinary forgetting" fails to occur (2008). Traumatic experiences that threaten to overwhelm an individual's mental state are split off and then remain unavailable to be worked on and modified into a symbol of the experience that can be retained as a memory in the mind. In such a situation, a later event may trigger a link to the traumatic experience with the result that the associated feelings and memories erupt with as great a force as the original live experience.

Segal made a differentiation between symbols proper and symbolic equations. In the symbolic equation the symbol is felt to be the same as the original object and is treated as though it is the original object. The true symbol, on the other hand, is recognized as having its own characteristics separate from that which it symbolizes; the symbolic equation is only partially separated and it remains involved with the same conflicts and inhibitions. Segal wrote,

> the symbol proper is felt to represent the object; its own characteristics are respected and used. It arises … when separation from the object, ambivalence, guilt and loss can be experienced and tolerated. The symbol is used not to deny but to overcome loss.
>
> (Segal, 1957, p. 395)

The Movement between the Paranoid–Schizoid and Depressive Positions

Klein pointed out the to-and-fro between the depressive and the paranoid–schizoid positions. In the depressive position we begin to face aspects of ourselves that make us guilty and anxious and when these feelings threaten to overwhelm us, we fall back into paranoid–schizoid ways of thinking. We see this in our patients and we can see it too in ourselves when we begin to learn things about ourselves that are hard to recognize and we can then find ourselves falling back into old ways of thinking or find ourselves blaming someone else. The essential point is the degree of fluidity between the positions, problems arise when paranoid–schizoid defences are held onto with rigidity and leave us impermeable to information from the external world.

Nowadays analysts tend to think less in terms of achieving and maintaining a depressive state of mind but more in terms of there being a fluctuation between the two states of mind. We may function mostly in one or other state of mind, but within this there will be moment to moment fluctuations. Analysts today will observe how a patient's state of mind changes from moment to moment in a session. Britton (2001) has argued that minute-to-minute fluctuations are an essential part of being alive and open to new development. New ideas can cause us to lose balance; we lose the sense of security that is provided by knowing how things are and this causes a sort of mental storm. Britton made the point that having our way of thinking disrupted is an inevitable and necessary aspect of taking in new and different ideas. He suggested that an uninterrupted state of balance and security is pathological and prevents development. His ideas link to Bion's (1970) idea of 'patience' and 'security' – security being the safety of the all-knowing paranoid–schizoid state and 'patience' being the capacity to bear uncertainty and confusion.

The Retreat from the Anxieties of Both Positions

A further addition to thinking about the movement between the positions is the idea of psychic retreat introduced by Steiner (1993). Building on the concept of the pathological organization, Steiner summed up his earlier thoughts in the chapter "The paranoid–schizoid and depressive positions" in which he described the way in which patients organize their defences in order to avoid the painful emotions and difficulties of both positions. He suggested that patients withdraw or retreat into a defensive state that maintains them in a state of emotional equilibrium.

In 1989 Britton wrote about what he called an "oedipal illusion" – a kind of retreat in which the patient believes himself to be the loved primary other; for example, in analysis he will believe that he is the most important figure in his analyst's life. This defence protects the patient against experiencing his murderous psychic reality, by which I mean his murderous feelings towards his analyst. Britton made the point that it is important to help the patient face the hated reality that he is outside the couple. He argued that the link between the parents provides the infant with a container with its own separate point of view from which he can be seen, known and thought about. This viewpoint, when internalized, provides the infant with a "third position" from which he can view himself. An individual able to look at himself from an outside point of view is better able to assess his own beliefs.

Britton warned that some patients find it very hard, if not impossible, to be thought about and he suggested that for these patients the thinker or the analyst is experienced as being in a sexual relationship (with his own thoughts or others in his mind) from which the patient feels horribly excluded. Steiner (2011) later elaborated on the painful feelings of shame and humiliation that can be experienced when we emerge from a psychic retreat and are seen for who and what we are; it is difficult when we have believed ourselves to be something that we are not.

I would like to use an example from a discussion that I wrote on a relational psychoanalysis in which I suggested that the model of working made it difficult for the analyst to sufficiently separate herself from her patient. I thought that the patient and analyst avoided the patient's extreme feelings by becoming a pair who ganged up against someone towards whom the patient felt envy and jealousy – her daughter's mother-in-law. The analyst asked the patient to show her a photo of the mother-in-law's handbag on her phone.

> Together we looked at it, admired it, looked up its price, and laughed together. While defending against envy, we became allies in her (the patient's) treatment. She started coming into sessions ready to show me what expensive clothes the mother-in-law wore, her newest model car, and the graduation present from the fanciest store for one of her grandchildren. Together we looked at photos on her phone and admired – or sometimes shared our feelings about the mother-in-law's awful taste. We had fun being envious as a team.
>
> (Kwalwasser, 2020, pp. 675–676)

The writer saw this as a developmental step that enabled the patient's envious feelings to be accepted and detoxified. From my point of view, I thought that the analyst was drawn into an enactment in which she and the patient became an observing pair, the mother-in-law being the one who was looked at and analysed. Rather than feeling shut out of the mind of her analyst when the analyst was thinking about her, the patient and the analyst joined together to think about the mother-in-law. Feelings of jealousy and envy did not have to be borne. The patient and her analyst were part of a pair that looked at, and also down, on someone else, an outlet for murderous feelings; a way of managing her paranoid anxieties.

> In looking down on the mother-in-law, the analyst could be experienced by the patient as joining her in the belief that locating inferiority in someone else and laughing at them, solves the problem. Together the analyst and patient can agree that the difficult situation of being outside the pair and observed; a situation that contains humiliating feelings of being inferior and terrifying anxieties about being seen as utterly worthless, can be got rid of. The analyst patient activity reinforces the belief that the difficult developmental step of accommodating these feelings within oneself can be avoided; the feelings can be evacuated into someone else and, best of all, the activity can be enjoyed.
>
> (Garvey, 2020, pp. 692–693)

To sum up

The shift from a paranoid–schizoid to a depressive position mental state is fraught with anxiety, guilt and painful feelings of loss, but if these can be tolerated it opens up the possibility of development and strengthens us to live in the real world. In a depressive state of mind, we can take in good aspects of others and try to develop similar good aspects in ourselves. This is a much slower developmental process than omnipotent introjective identification in which we magically and instantly possess whatever skills and knowledge we want to have and are rid of those aspects of ourselves that we prefer to be without.

The individual in a depressive position state of mind knows more or less who and what he is and what he is not and has a realistic awareness of his limits. He does not confuse himself with his object, does not attribute aspects of himself to his object nor claim aspects of his object for himself. Realistic identifications give us the strength to bear guilt and to make reparation.

References

Bion, W. (1970) *Attention and Interpretation*. London: Tavistock.

Britton, R. (2001) Beyond the depressive position: Ps(n+1), in C. Bronstein (ed.), *Kleinian Theory: A Contemporary Perspective*. London: Whurr, pp. 63–76.

Britton, R. (1989) The missing link: Parental sexuality in the Oedipus complex, in *The Oedipus Complex Today: Clinical Implications*. London: Karnac, pp. 83–101.

Britton, R. (1998) Daydream, phantasy and fiction, in *Belief and Imagination: Explorations in Psychoanalysis*. London: Routledge, pp. 109–119.

Britton, R. (2018) The mountains of primal grief, in P. Garvey & K. Long (eds.), *The Klein Tradition*. London: Routledge, pp. 113–123.

Freud, S. (1917) Mourning and melancholia, *S.E.* 14. London: Hogarth Press, pp. 237–258.

Freud, S. (1930) Civilisation and its discontents. *S.E.* 21: 59–148.

Garvey, P. (2020) A discussion of "Whose envy is it anyway?", *Psychoanalytic Dialogues* 30: 689–693.

Klein, M. (1927) Criminal tendencies in normal children, in *The Writings of Melanie Klein*, vol. 1. London: Hogarth Press, pp. 170–185.

Klein, M. (1935) A contribution to the psychogenesis of manic-depressive states, in *The Writings of Melanie Klein*, vol. 1. London: Hogarth Press, pp. 262–289.

Klein, M. (1940) Mourning and its relation to manic-depressive states, in *The Writings of Melanie Klein*, vol. 1. London: Hogarth Press, pp. 344–369.

Klein, M. (1945) The Oedipus complex in the light of early anxieties, in *The Writings of Melanie Klein*, vol. 1. London: Hogarth Press, pp. 370–419.

Klein, M. (1946) Notes on some schizoid mechanisms, in *The Writings of Melanie Klein*, vol. 3. London: Hogarth Press, pp. 1–24.

Kwalwasser, L. (2020) Whose envy is it anyway?, *Psychoanalytic Dialogues*, 30: 666–681.

O'Shaughnessy, E. (2018) Reparation: Waiting for a concept, in P. Garvey & K. Long (eds.), *The Klein Tradition*. London: Routledge, pp. 199–203.

Rilke, R. M. (1969) *Letters of Rainer Maria Rilke* (B. Greene & H. Norton (trans., eds.). New York: W. W. Norton.

Segal, H. (1957) Some aspects of the analysis of a schizophrenic. *International Journal of Psycho-Analysis*, 38: 391–397; republished in *The Work of Hanna Segal*. New York: Jason Aronson, pp. 49–65.

Segal, H. (1974) Delusion and artistic creativity: Some reflections on reading The Spire by William Golding. *International Review of Psycho-Analysis*, 1: 135–141.

Sodre, I. (2008) Where lights and shadows fall, in H. Harvey-Wood & A. S. Byatt (eds.), *Memory: An Anthology*. London: Chatto & Windus.

Steiner, J. (1993) The paranoid–schizoid and depressive positions, in *Psychic Retreats*. London: Routledge, pp. 25–39.

Steiner, J. (2011) *Seeing and Being Seen: Emerging from a Psychic Retreat*. London: Routledge.

Chapter 5

Internal Objects, the Superego and Its Destructive Potential

Overview of Concept of Superego

The superego has a long and complex history. In his 1933 paper "Dissection of the psychical personality", Freud wrote:

> patients who suffer from delusions of being observed might 'be right' and that in each of us there is present in his ego an agency like this which observes and threatens to punish and, which in them, has merely become sharply divided from their ego and mistakenly displaced into external reality.

This agency had earlier been named the superego; a part of the self that is commonly equated with the conscience, that oversees, judges, guides, supports, controls and criticizes. It contains both the aspirations and the restriction of the parents, but it is not always a support, and it can cause a lot of trouble, in part because it contains the parents' ideals rather than their aspirations and in part because it is a gathering place for the death instincts (Freud, 1923).

In an earlier paper "Mourning and melancholia" (1917), Freud had already outlined a particular kind of destructive internal relationship caused by the complex identifications that take place when hatred and rage against the separated object interfere with mourning its loss. He explained the way in which one part of the self is identified with the hated lost object. The individual takes in and identifies part of himself with the loved lost object while another part, full of rage against the loved abandoning object,

DOI: 10.4324/9781003215714-6

turns its hostility and condemnation against the part of the self that is identified with that once loved, but now hated, object. Freud thought of the condemning aspect of the self as a precursor to the superego, a part of the self that condemns the self.

For Klein the early harsh internal object is an early superego and is an expected feature in normal development. Once Klein had adopted Freud's idea of the death instinct, the early terrifyingly bad object was not only retaliatory but also contained the split-off death instinct with its destructive and self-destructive urges. As if this was not enough, Klein argued that not all death instinct is projected out by the infant into the object; some remains within and is internally projected into the superego where it can be safely contained and where it provides the superego with the strength and power it needs for the exercise of control.

Klein concluded that an early superego exists almost from birth. Here her theory deviates radically from that of Freud. Freud's superego is a later development, resulting from the resolution of the Oedipus complex. Klein's superego precedes this resolution and is a central and live participant in the turmoil of extreme desires and feelings. Klein's superego is a version of the id, as it is formed at base from the extreme primitive unmodified instincts of life and death. In Klein's theory the extremely good and extremely bad introjected objects are from the start installed within both the ego and the superego, and in a later addition to her theory (1958), they are also relegated to the deep unconscious where they remain out of contact with reality. In a healthy individual these figures erupt into consciousness only when under extreme stress, but for others, less developmentally strong, whether due to constitutional weakness or insufficient good experience, these figures may be much more disruptive.

Modification of the Superego

Klein viewed the early harsh superego as normal, and she reasoned that over time with sufficient repeated good experience it will become modified due to interaction with the outside world and with the ego. In this situation the ego is sufficiently strong and is not overwhelmed by anxiety. When life instinct predominates over death instinct, the extreme hostile and loving aspects of the self and other come together, the object and self become closer, and as the good and bad are seen as being one and the same, they become less extreme. But some people continue to be persecuted by a tormenting superego, a superego that fails to modify. Klein and others struggled to work out how and why it was that they found themselves working with patients whose persecution remained unmodified or who remained impervious from contact with the analyst. They repeatedly came up against something in their patients that seemed to be unalterable.

Threading through her papers Klein went over questions about the degree to which psychoanalysis could alter the primary internal objects – and for her this meant the superego as she thought of it as very much composed of primary objects. In 1927 she wrote "I am led to believe from the analysis of children that their super-ego is a highly resistant product, at heart unalterable" (Klein, 1927, p. 155). In 1929 she stated that the early severe superego could modify but in 1933 she argued that, even so, "analysis can never entirely do away with the sadistic nucleus of the superego" (Klein, 1933, p. 256). Freud concluded in 1937 that innate destructiveness limits what psychoanalysis is able to achieve but in 1952 Klein sounded more optimistic and referred to the "progressive assimilation of the superego by the ego" (Klein, 1952, p. 74) and, in notes on this same paper, she elaborated that "infantile persecutory anxieties can be fully experienced, worked through and diminished if the patient can transfer the frightening figures onto the psycho-analyst".

In 1958 when Klein introduced the idea of the extreme objects being relegated to the deep unconscious, she came up with a solution that allows for both modification – the modification of the objects in the ego and superego – and un-alterability – the un-alterability of the objects in the deep unconscious. She explained that this was caused by the defusion of the life and death instincts due to the pressure of anxiety. Early extremely dangerous emotions need to be kept safely away from more loving ones.

> The difference in these two ways of splitting … is that in the splitting-off of frightening figures defusion seems to be in the ascendent; whereas super-ego formation is carried out with a predominance of fusion of the two instincts. Therefore the

super-ego is normally established in close relation with the ego and shares different aspects of the same good objects. This makes it possible for the ego to integrate and accept the super-ego to a greater or less extent. In contrast the extremely bad figures are not accepted by the ego in this way and are constantly rejected by it.

(Klein, 1958, p. 241)

Analysts found that some patients were stuck in the kind of melancholic state described by Freud whereas others exhibited a more overtly superior state. One strand of thinking about these states started with Riviere's 1936 paper on the negative therapeutic reaction in which she wrote about "a highly organised system of defence". Riviere based her theory on Klein's 1935 ideas about the manic defences against the anxieties of the depressive position – defences such as the omnipotent denial of dependence and guilt, and the contemptuous devaluation of the object. Klein and others thought that damaged internal objects persecuted the patient from within.

The contrast between persecutory and idealized, between good and bad objects – being an expression of life and death instincts and forming the basis of phantasy life – is to be found in every layer of the self. Among the hated and threatening objects, which the early ego tries to ward off, are also those which are felt to have been injured or killed and which thereby turn into dangerous persecutors.

(Klein, 1958, p. 241)

Rosenfeld (1952), thinking along similar lines, wrote about an "ego-splitting superego" an internal persecutor fragmenting the individual from within. Many others also wrote about intractable states in which the patient seems to be dominated by a powerful internal figure who prevents him from taking in anything good from his analyst or from anyone else. This anti-developmental force or anti-life force is often referred to as a kind of superego – a superego dominated by the death instinct. Klein herself wrote about an "envious superego" (1957) and Bion (1959) referred to an "ego-destructive" superego.

The unmodified persecuting superego can drive the individual to suicide as is well described by Ted Hughes (1998) in his poem "The blue flannel suit", in which he described seeing the torment experienced by his wife, Sylvia Plath, when giving her first lecture. She was later to kill herself.

> … Now I know, as I did not,
> What eyes waited at the back of the class
> To check your first professional performance
> Against their expectations. What assessors
> Waited to see you justify the cost
> And redeem their gamble. What a furnace
> Of yes waited to prove your metal …
> … You waited,
> Knowing yourself helpless in the tweezers
> Of the life that judged you …

Pathological Organization of the Personality

Rosenfeld took a particular interest in the kind of organized defensive system described by Riviere and, writing later than her, he based his thoughts on Klein's ideas of paranoid–schizoid defences with a powerful figure at the centre of what he called a "narcissistic organisation". The dominant figure is frequently thought of as a kind of superego – or in Bion's words a "super ego". The superego imprisons the vulnerable dependent part of the personality and prevents it from making links with anyone outside himself who might be helpful. Such an individual wants to be the most powerful person around and often the most valuable and important one. In order to achieve this, he has to destroy everything or everyone else who is of value or who threatens his position of power. At the same time, he denies all vulnerable, and therefore real and human, aspects of himself. Rosenfeld (1971), Meltzer (1968) and Steiner (1982, 1987), whose term "pathological organizations" has been adopted as descriptive of this group of patients, have written extensively on this kind of internal dynamic. In his 1971 paper Rosenfeld provided a patient's dream which is much quoted because it gives a vivid illustration of the internal dynamics:

A small boy was in a comatose condition, dying from some kind of poisoning. He was in the sun which was beginning to shine on him. The patient was standing near to the boy in the shade but did nothing to move or protect him. He only felt critical and superior to the doctor treating the child, since it was he who should have seen that the child was moved into the shade.

(Rosenfeld, 1971, p. 174)

The dying vulnerable part of the patient is maintained in its dying position, the patient critically observes and does not lift a finger to help (himself). The perverse nature of the internal relationship is important because the gratification derived from thwarting the provider of help plays a significant part in keeping the organization in place.

A patient who rejected almost everything that I said, surprised me one day by whispering, just as she was leaving my consulting room, "you were right about what you said". I wondered who it was that was not meant to hear what she had said to me. My thought was that a powerful figure inside her would not allow her to take in anything from me, insisted that she was perfectly alright as she was, and told her that she knew everything that there was to know about herself. The superior internal figure did not permit her to be deficient in any way. A part of her knew that she needed what I had to offer but had to manage the internal omnipotent and omniscient one who was not to know that she had anything to learn from me. This kind of powerful superego is destructive of learning and development, its harshness and severity may be directed outwards or inwards, usually it is both, it attacks the vulnerable undeveloped self who is hated for its imperfections and inadequacy and attacks also the competent other in possession of needed resources.

Envy

Some patients reject their analyst's good efforts and particularly do so when they are well understood. Klein arrived at the conclusion that envy plays a crucial part in the ability or inability to take in something good from another person. Envy and the death instinct are often spoken about together as though indistinguishable. Klein thought of envy as a manifestation of the death instinct. A manifestation, but not the only one, envy is an expression of the death instinct in action. Envy is not just about wanting to have it all for yourself, envy includes a hatred of anything good that we ourselves do not possess. An object or quality or capacity that we wish we had but that we do not possess provokes in all of us, to different degrees, a painful kind of desire. The pain of envy can promote a constructive desire to develop and to acquire the desired thing or to become like the loved one or, on the other hand, when envy cannot be borne, it may trigger an attempt to steal what is good or to attack and destroy it. The good thing that we do not have, or the possessor of the good thing, is hated. Envy causes good things to turn bad. The Dementors who appear in J. K. Rowling's (1999) Harry Potter series of children's books seem to me to be an embodiment of envy; they are described as sucking the happiness out of a situation. They do this by attacking the good-loved object and can only be resisted by massive effort.

If we receive something good but we are filled with envy of the person who is giving it to us, we will take in something bad, or will take in the good thing mixed with hatred for the giver. So, in Kleinian terms, rather than taking in a good object, the envious individual takes in a bad object – an object that provokes bad feelings and disturbs the individual from inside. In this malign cycle the individual may end up with a sense of having inside himself a mother or analyst who hates him and wants to strip him of all goodness. Envy interferes with our being able to take in a good experience.

An excess of envy or inability to bear the pain of not having knowledge is a handicap to learning; we need to be able to suffer our own lack of knowledge if we are to be able to take in something unknown. Some people will find it easier to learn from books, as they may find it particularly painful to be exposed to another person who already possesses the knowledge that they do not. A supervisee of mine who had great difficulty in being open to my ideas said to me "the trouble is that sometimes you see things that I have not yet seen". My capacity to see things that she had not yet seen was not felt by her to be something good that she could use for her own development, but rather it was experienced as a difficulty that had to be suffered. I am not sure whether she thought the suffering was worth it or whether it was felt to be without any advantage. Another patient, who was dominated by a powerful omniscient internal object, returned from a summer holiday and told me that he had been snorkelling with his children and had found it very difficult to bear it when they saw fish that he had not yet seen; he said to me "I had to see them first". In 1962 Bion referred to this state of mind as –K and wrote that "The most important characteristic is its hatred of any new development in the personality as if the new development were a rival to be destroyed" (Bion, 1962, p. 98).

Envy is to be distinguished from greed and jealousy. Greed is wanting it all for yourself and it does not necessarily concern a relationship with another person – it can be about people or food or money or other things. It is about wanting to have more than you need or can use. The greedy person may enjoy what they have at the time, but they are never satisfied. Greed may be caused by deprivation and by the anxiety that an offer of resources may be the last chance that there is to acquire them. Greed is increased by anxiety, and greed will itself lead to anxiety. Jealousy involves the experience of being left out of a couple, being on the outside of a loving relationship and having to bear the awareness of someone else receiving the love that you want for yourself; it is a very painful experience that involves other people.

Klein had the idea that the mother may be experienced by her infant as deliberately withholding that which is desired, the mother is experienced as greedily keeping it all for herself. It is important to discriminate between situations where something is in fact being withheld and situations dominated by envy in which the possessor, however generous or fair a giver, is seen as mean and withholding. This sense of something being greedily withheld is often accompanied by a sense of entitlement in which the individual argues that what is being withheld is rightfully his. This configuration underlies many situations of grievance. You can see this kind of thing reflected in political situations – e.g. Trump's "the election was stolen". Some elections are stolen, others are not. But when the loss cannot be borne, mourning is replaced by righteous anger at the those who possesses the thing we want. Political leaders may themselves be full of grievance and certainly frequently play on the envy and grievance in the population in order to arouse loyalty to themselves and to stir up hatred and violence against any who oppose them, often with disastrous consequences, even war. A leader unable to come to terms with the limits of his power and a suffering population or one unable to bear losses, such as the loss of empire or earlier greatness, are a lethal combination.

Primitive feelings of aggrieved omnipotence can be stirred up in all of us when we find ourselves up against limits to the satisfaction of our desires; we can feel that we have a right to have and do whatever we wish, we should not be limited. The envious person cannot bear to not possess that which they want. In a paper on grievance, Michael Feldman argued that grievance can be the result of a failure to resolve oedipal desires. He explained that the individual may believe that he was promised that he would be his mother's favourite for ever and that he feels that the promise has been broken – he has been betrayed (2008).

Reaction to the Idea of Envy

When Klein introduced the idea of an inborn tendency to enviously attack goodness it was met with horror and many analysts remain shocked at the idea that anyone could think of an infant as being full of destructive envy. Whatever is the case with babies, I think it is hard to avoid being aware of envy in our ordinary lives and its destructive nature. In clinical work envy interferes with a patient's capacity to benefit from therapy or analysis – or indeed any good experiences or opportunities that they are offered. Klein's successors built on her ideas of envy and there is agreement that the degree of a patient's envy is of considerable significance in their capacity or incapacity to improve.

Clinical Example

I will give an example of a patient who contained a powerfully harsh ego-destructive superego. At the outset Mrs B described herself in an idealized way. She explained that she was entirely unselfish and was able to be this way because she could do without, she was stronger than anyone else. It became clear that somewhere in her imagination she thought of herself as Jesus Christ and when I put this to her, she began to giggle. It was obvious to us both that I was right.

She had been born into a family with its own manufacturing and retail business in a busy city. The family suffered a very painful tragedy that left a deep emotional scar on them all – and I think had caused her mother not only to be depressed but also very anxious about Mrs B's welfare. The mother felt that her child was very vulnerable and that she had to be protected from disturbance. At the same time, I think that Mrs B felt that her mother was very vulnerable, and she had to protect her from any disturbing feelings. The father was presented as manly, unfeeling and with a tendency to intrude horrible violent reality into the situation – not that he was actively violent. I had the impression that Mrs B and her mother attempted to live in a cocoon together in which each believed that the survival of the other depended on her. Separation from her mother was not possible, there were echoes of this dynamic in significant other relationships in her life. My understanding was that Mrs B was paralyzed by a fear of destroying her objects. Her liveliness was severely impaired, and her aggression and violence were split off. I think that Mrs B believed herself to be enormously powerful, loved the sense of power but was also terrified of it and very afraid that she had been the cause of the family tragedy.

I think that Mrs B was in an omnipotent identification with her mother; she was the baby with the breast and her vulnerability was projected into her mother. She did not have to nor could she separate herself from her mother. She did not have to give up anything as she believed herself to possesses all the desirable qualities of the other. At times during her life, I think she had believed that things were just the way that she wanted them to be, but at other times she sensed that she was missing out and had missed out on a lot. At times she was her own ego ideal and felt (precariously) enormously loved by herself and by her superego. There was though, a 'bad' threatening reality in the form of the father, possibly life itself and a reality sense of her own.

Frequently when Mrs B gained some knowledge in the analysis of a lively emotional self, she heard a voice inside her head that said, "you would be better off on your own". One year, just before I was leaving to go away for a four-week summer holiday, Mrs B told me that the voice inside her head said, "you can always kill yourself". She told me that the voice had nothing to do with my holiday and nothing at all to do with me – in general she thought I ascribed too much importance to myself. However, the voice told her to kill herself outside my consulting room – and this made it obvious to me and eventually to her that it did have something to do with me. My understanding was that she was worried about how she was going to manage without me, that she was angry with me for mattering enough to cause her to feel something about my absence, and was furious at not being able to control me or control her own feelings. I think she wanted to disturb me and get me back under her control. I was to believe that her survival depended on me and therefore be too frightened to separate from her. She also wanted to kill off what she felt was an inferior part of herself that had feelings, and without doubt she also wanted to punish me.

With difficulty on the Friday session of the week in which this voice appeared, Mrs B acknowledged the link that I made between her suicidal threats and my holiday. She said that she did feel some anger towards me. She began to express her anger and told me that *she* would never treat a fragile patient in the way that I was intending to treat her. The voice continued to suggest that she kill herself; I felt menaced. I found it hard to judge just how seriously to take this; I was worried that Mrs B might be suffi- ciently dissociated not to appreciate that killing herself involved killing all of herself. I wondered whether she realized that she could not just get rid of the inferior unwanted part and live on in a superior state. I did not know how far she might go in her determination to get rid of her inferior emotional self and take revenge on me. I was anxious over the weekend, and I decided that, on Monday, I would talk to Mrs B about the possibility that she, but if not she then I, should take her state seriously and con- tact her doctor and ask that she be available to see her during my absence. Mrs B arrived on the Monday morning in a better state;

she said that I had been right about her anger and that it had meant a lot to her that I had recognized it, that I had stood the anxiety and that I had not given in to her. She said that all her life she had been overprotected, given in to, treated as weak and allowed to get away with not doing difficult things. She regretted that while growing up she had been allowed to miss out on so much of normal life.

Suicide, Near Death States and the Death Instinct

Don Campbell and Rob Hale (2017) have drawn attention to many aspects of the pre-suicidal mind and the lethal combination of a murderous persecutor and a guilty victim in the mind of a suicidal patient. I was a guilty murderer leaving a vulnerable patient, but Mrs. B too was a guilty murderer whose murderous feelings towards me should be killed. The title of Bell's 2001 paper, "Who is killing what or whom", draws attention to the importance of identifying the internal dynamics. Bion (1959) wrote that analysis gives the patient the opportunity to explore himself in a personality that is powerful enough to contain him. I had reached the limits of my capacity to tolerate anxiety and even though my survival did not depend on that of Mrs B, it would have been emotionally difficult for me to survive her suicide. I think that it helped that I was able to face the limits of my power and to recognize that I could not save her on my own. I was not Jesus Christ – not as powerful nor as good nor selfless. I did not have to be captive to my superego ideal, I could face being limited and ask for help.

Rosenfeld 1971 warned that some patients will kill themselves rather than face the limits of their power and he also drew attention to the perverse seductive pull towards suicide in which the act is depicted as a pain-free way of escape. One patient frequently spoke dreamily and positively about killing himself by walking into the sea. This was spoken about as though it would be a peaceful and almost blissful experience. The perverse nature of the internal relationship between the different parts of the self has been flagged up by many writers who note the way in which the vulnerable emotional part of the individual seems to be a willing captive of the superior one who offers death as an ideal solution. The patient's dissociation from reality and from the real pain and consequences of killing themselves puts them in danger. The pain and guilt are of course left in those who remain behind.

For some patients, the aim is not to kill themselves but to keep themselves alive in a near death state. The idea of the psychic equilibrium of near death – a state in which all disturbing emotions are kept at bay – has been investigated in detail by a number of analysts and pre-eminently by Betty Joseph, who brought close attention to the way in which the projective and introjective processes involved can be observed as they play out in the minutiae of the interaction between analyst and patient in the clinical situation. In her paper "Addiction to near death" (1982), Joseph drew attention to the satisfaction derived by the patient from thwarting the analyst and preventing development. Feldman has also written extensively on this topic and in his paper on the death instinct (2000) he details the way in which attacks on meaning, on clarity and on any creative thought are used by the patient to prevent development and keep the analyst and patient in a near death state. This situation is likened to the relationship between a torturer and his victim, the torturer does not want to kill the victim but wants to keep him alive so that he can continue to inflict pain.

There remains some disagreement about how to define the death instinct: is it, as in Feldman's definition, an instinct that derives satisfaction from preventing development or is it one that drives towards death or at least the annihilation of the capacity to take in experience? A further question is the degree to which it is defensive and protects against a potentially overwhelming experience – rather along the lines of Ferenczi's idea that every living organism reacts to unpleasant stimuli by fragmentation. Segal describes the death instinct in the following way:

> Birth confronts us with the experience of needs. In relation to that experience there can be two reactions, and both, I think, are invariably present in all of us though in varying proportions. One, to seek satisfaction for the needs: that is life-promoting and leads to object seeking, love and eventually object

concern. The other is the drive to annihilate: the need to annihilate the perceiving experiencing self as well as anything that is perceived.

(Segal, 1997, p. 24)

As analysts, our aim where possible is to strengthen the individual to bear the pain of life. Among the many things that this involves is the loosening of the hold of the destructive superego. The superior figure needs to be subjected to scrutiny and questioning, unrealistic demands for perfection must been seen for what they are – destructive attacks. In Britton's words "we must not simply be judged by our conscience; we must submit our conscience to judgement" (2003, p. 101). There is some debate as to whether the one that makes realistic judgements is still a superego – a modified, depressive position superego – or whether it is the ego. Britton suggested that this latter judge is the ego, whereas for O'Shaughnessy (1999) it is a 'normal' as opposed to an 'abnormal' superego. It is a superego that names a crime but does so in a manner in which the crime can be known and dealt with. Such a superego should provide the individual with understanding and with support to become better, do better, where possible make things better and where not possible provide support for sadness and regret. An abnormal superego is, in the terms of Chris Mawson and Donna Savary in a yet to be published book, not a superego at all but a Godlike creature that holds out no hope and offers only condemnation.

References

Bell, D. (2001) Who is killing what or whom? Some notes on the internal phenomenology of suicide. *Psychoanalytic Psychotherapy*, 15: 21–37.

Bion, W. (1959) Attacks on linking. *International Journal of Psycho-Analysis*, 40: 308–315.

Bion, W. (1962) *Learning from Experience*. London: Heinemann Medical Books, Ch. 28.

Britton, R. (2003) *Sex, Death and the Superego*. London: Karnac.

Campbell, D. & Hale, R. (2017) *Working in the Dark: Understanding the Pre-Suicide State of Mind*. London: Routledge.

Feldman, M. (2000) Some views on the manifestation of the death instinct in clinical work. *International Journal of Psycho-Analysis*, 81: 53–65.

Feldman, M. (2008) Grievance: The underlying Oedipal configuration. *International Journal of Psycho-Analysis*, 89: 743–758.

Freud, S. (1917) Mourning and melancholia, *S.E.* 14. London: Hogarth Press, pp. 237–258.

Freud, S. (1923) The ego and the id, *S.E.* 19. London: Hogarth Press, pp. 3–66.

Freud, S. (1933) The dissection of the psychical personality, *S.E.* 22. London: Hogarth Press, pp. 57–80.

Freud, S. (1937) Analysis terminable and interminable, *S.E.* 23. London: Hogarth Press, pp. 209–253.

Hughes, T. (1998) The blue flannel suit, in *Birthday Letters.* London: Faber & Faber.

Joseph, B. (1982) Addiction to near death. *International Journal of Psycho-Analysis*, 63: 449–456.

Klein, M. (1927) Symposium on child analysis, in *The Writings of Melanie Klein*, Vol. 1. London: Hogarth Press, pp. 139–169.

Klein, M. (1929) Personification in the play of children, in *The Writings of Melanie Klein*, vol. 1. London: Hogarth Press, pp. 199–209.

Klein, M. (1933) The early development of conscience in the child, in *The Writings of Melanie Klein*, vol. 1. London: Hogarth Press, pp. 248–257.

Klein, M. (1935) A contribution to the psychogenesis of manic-depressive states, in *The Writings of Melanie Klein*, vol. 1. London: Hogarth Press, pp. 262–289.

Klein, M. (1952) Some theoretical conclusions regarding the emotional life of the infant, in *The Writings of Melanie Klein*, vol. 3. London: Hogarth Press, pp. 61–93.

Klein, M. (1957) Envy and gratitude, in *The Writings of Melanie Klein*, vol. 3. London: Hogarth Press, pp. 176–235.

Klein, M. (1958) On the development of mental functioning, in *The Writings of Melanie Klein*, vol. 3. London: Hogarth Press, pp. 236–246.

Mawson, C. & Savary, D. *The Mind's God-Like Voice: Psychoanalytic Observations of Narcissism, Echoism, and the Destruction of the Ego* (unpublished).

Meltzer, D. (1968) Terror, persecution and dread. *International Journal of Psycho-Analysis*, 49: 396–400.

O'Shaughnessy, E. (1999) Relating to the superego, *International Journal of Psycho-Analysis*, 80: 861–870.

Riviere, J. (1936) A contribution to the analysis of the negative therapeutic reaction. *International Journal of Psycho-Analysis*, 17: 304–320.

Rosenfeld, H. (1952) Notes on the psycho-analysis of the super-ego conflict of an acute schizophrenic patient. *International Journal of Psycho-Analysis*, 33: 111–131.

Rosenfeld, H. (1971) A clinical approach to the psychoanalytic theory of the life and death instincts: An investigation into the aggressive aspects of narcissism. *International Journal of Psycho-Analysis*, 52: 169–178.

Rowling, J. K. (1999) *Harry Potter and the Prisoner of Azkaban*. London: Bloomsbury.

Segal, H. (1997) On the clinical usefulness of the concept of the death instinct, in J. Steiner (ed.), *Psychoanalysis, Literature and War*. London: Routledge, pp. 17–26.

Steiner, J. (1982) Perverse relationships between parts of the self: A clinical illustration. *International Journal of Psycho-Analysis*, 63: 241–251.

Steiner, J. (1987) The interplay between pathological organizations and the paranoid–schizoid and depressive positions. *International Journal of Psycho-Analysis*, 68: 69–80.

Chapter 6

Technique, Projective and Introjective Identification and Countertransference

Klein on Transference, Countertransference and Interpretation

Transference

Freud famously wrote:

> This struggle between the doctor and the patient, between intellect and instinctual life, between understanding and seeking to act, is played out almost exclusively in the phenomena of transference. It is on that field that the victory must be won … For when all is said and done, it is impossible to destroy anyone *in absentia* or *in effigie*.
>
> (Freud, 1912a, p. 108)

Klein agreed with Freud's words; she understood that children and all of us are full of powerful loving and hostile feelings that have existed within us from the start of our lives, that these take the form of unconscious and conscious phantasies/ fantasies in the inner world and that particular aspects of both past and current emotional relationships are transferred and played out in the transference with the analyst at different times. Klein treated anything that was said or brought into the session as revealing of the patient's relationship with her, she attended to the whole situation (1952), not just to remarks that were about her.

DOI: 10.4324/9781003215714-7

Countertransference

Klein was aware that infants affect their mothers and the relationship that develops between them. In a similar way, patients affect how their analysts feel and also how they behave, and this in turn affects the patient:

> However, it is not only the infant's feelings about the external world are coloured by his projection, but the mother's actual relation to her child is in indirect and subtle ways, influenced by the infant's response to her. A contented baby who sucks with enjoyment, allays this mother's anxiety; and her happiness expresses itself in her way of handling and feeding him, thus diminishing his persecutory anxiety and affecting his ability to internalise the good breast. In contrast, a child who has difficulties over feeding may arouse the mother's anxiety and guilt and thus unfavourably influence her relation to him.
>
> (Klein, 1963, p. 312)

Klein strongly believed that the analyst must take care not to allow the patient to overwhelm her but must rather hold onto her feelings and think about them. Klein did not explicitly state that the analyst needs to contain the patient's feelings, but she described a process in which the analyst manages because she is interested in how the mind works, because she knows about projective identification and because she understands the inevitability of transference feelings from the patient, including negative ones. It is this understanding that makes it easier for the analyst to bear her countertransference:

> Really the patient violently wants to put himself into the analyst to get mixed up with him and to put all his depression, aggression, violence and so on, into the analysis. ... Up to a point one is influenced by that, I mean, it is not as if one is not absolutely without response to it, one feels that it is happening.
>
> [...]

But the effect can be limited and can be kept much better under control by knowledge of what projective identification is and that it is part of the patient's illness.

(Klein, 1958 in Steiner, 2017, p. 113)

But Klein did not place her main focus on, nor explore in great detail, the processes that take place inside the analyst or inside the mother. Much of her attention was on the internal and constitutional aspects of the patient or infant as she thought that environmental factors were sufficiently acknowledged:

But … the importance of internal factors is still underrated, destructive impulses, varying from individual to individual, are an integral part of mental life, even in favourable circumstances, and therefore we have to consider the development of the child and the attitudes of the adults as resulting from the interaction between internal and external influences … The struggle between love and hate … can to some extent be recognised through careful observation, some babies experience strong resentment about any frustration and show this by being unable to accept gratification when it follows on deprivation.

(Klein, 1959, p. 249)

Klein's emphasis on internal factors has led many to conclude, quite wrongly, that she laid no importance on mothering or the environment, and yet time and again she mentioned the importance of the mothering that a child receives and, given that she worked as a psychoanalyst, she must have thought that an external relationship has the potential to modify the internal world.

Technique

Klein thought that it is important to interpret at the point of maximum urgency, she was aware that this is a point of intense anxiety for the patient and that the analyst needs to be able to tolerate the patient's anxiety if his feelings are to fully emerge. Klein saw that love is often buried under hate and that hate must be given a place in the relationship so that love and curiosity can be freed. She realized this had to be done step by step. She thought that care needed to be taken with the manner of raising these threatening topics. As you may imagine, an analyst talking to a patient about his jealousy or his fear of her, or of his envious wish to mess her up, might make him feel persecuted and accused. He might also feel accused if the analyst were to suggest that he is critical of her; he might fear that the analyst would be unable to think about the criticism and try to understand it and would be unable to bear accurate criticism. Furthermore, if the patient is afraid of the analyst, she might be the last person to whom he would want to reveal himself. Kleinian analysts have been frequently criticized for moving in too quickly to address aggression. Klein herself wrote that it is important to remember that the patient may be completely unaware that he has any unpleasant feelings about his analyst, as these unwanted feelings may be split off. She was clear that the manner and timing of bringing these negative feelings to the patient's attention needs careful thought:

> But it is essential not to attempt to hurry these steps in integration. For if the realization of the division in his personality were to come suddenly, the patient would have great difficulties in coping with it. The more strongly had the envious and destructive impulses been split off, the more dangerous the patient feels them to be when he becomes conscious of them. In analysis we should make our way slowly and gradually towards the painful insight into the divisions in the patient's self.
>
> (Klein, 1957, pp. 224–225)

Bion's Concept of Normal Projective Identification and Its Influence on Technique

It was Winnicott with his ideas about the mother's reverie and his idea about hate in the countertransference, and Bion with his development of the concept of projective identification and his theory of container contained, who brought focus and detail to what it is in a mother's attention that is emotionally transformative. Bion's is the work that has primarily influenced the thinking and technique of Klein's followers, although there is a growing interest in looking in greater detail at the similarities and differences between Klein and Winnicott. One example of this is the published conversation between Jan Abram and Bob Hinshelwood (2018) and a soon to be published conversation between them comparing the theories of Winnicott and Bion.

To give a brief outline of Bion's ideas, Bion concluded that infants and disturbed individuals are threatened by overwhelming feelings and that they need to communicate these feelings to someone else. The communication is achieved by the activity of projection in which the feelings are located in the other person. Bion argued that projection is a means of early, primitive communication and that the preverbal infant communicates by projecting and arousing his feelings – intense anxiety – in his mother or caretaker. For this Bion coined the term "normal projective identification"; an activity that he thought of as basic and necessary. Both Bion and Rosenfeld were working with psychotic patients and saw that these patients used projection into their analysts as a way of communicating their terrifying anxieties. They concluded that their patients had failed to develop the capacity of verbal communication and were employing the only means they could, preverbal 'normal' projective identification. Bion thought that these patients had been deprived, early in their lives, of the opportunity to project their feelings into another person able to take them in. It was his view that the patient experienced this denial as being in the presence of a projection-rejecting object. He reasoned that the patient had then internalized the object with the result that he had inside him an object that attacked his own and other people's attempts at communication (Bion, 1957, 1959). Bion placed his theories within Klein's theory of the death instinct and did not come down on the side of whether the fault lay with the mother or with the infant:

On the one hand there is the patient's inborn, disposition to excessive destructiveness, hatred, and envy: on the other the environment which, at its worst, denies to the patient the use of the mechanisms of splitting and projective identification. On some occasions the destructive attacks on the link between patient and environment, or between different aspects of the patient's personality, have their origin in the patient; on others, in the mother, although in the latter instance and in psychotic patients, it can never be in the mother alone.

(Bion, 1959, p. 313)

Bion concluded that good emotional and cognitive development depends on the experience of having a receptive mother or caretaker who takes in the projected anxieties, bears them, makes sense of them and responds in a manner that conveys understanding. The analyst also 'contains' the feelings and in doing so, the patient's anxiety and terror are detoxified and returned accompanied by thought or by proto-thought along with the sense of an object that has the capacity to think. Bion made the point that if we are to develop our cognitive and emotional capacities we need to have spent sufficient time in the presence of an individual with the emotional strength and capacity to take in and bear our projected feelings. Just as the infant needs a containing mother, the patient needs an analyst who can contain him:

Projective identification makes it possible for him to investigate his own feelings in a personality powerful enough to contain them.

(Bion, 1959, p. 314)

A version of this idea had been touched on much earlier by Freud (see Mawson, 2018 for a discussion of this):

It takes place by *extraneous help*, when the attention of an experienced person is drawn to the child's state by discharge along the path of internal change. In this way this path of discharge acquires a secondary function of the highest importance, that of *communication*, and the initial helplessness of human beings is the *primal source* of all *moral motives*. [By this Freud means social and group mentality.]

When the helpful person has performed the work of the specific action in the external world for the helpless one, the latter is in a position, by means of reflex contrivances, immediately to carry out in the interior of his body the activity necessary for removing the endogenous stimulus. The total event then constitutes an *experience of satisfaction*, which has the most radical result on the development of the individual's functions.

(Freud, 1950, p. 318, emphasis in original)

Countertransference

The widespread exploration of the mechanisms of projective identification, along with the interest in the phenomenon of countertransference, led to significant developments in technique. The term countertransference covers a wide range of phenomena. It is defined differently in different parts of the world and in different schools of thought. At first the term was used solely to refer to the analyst's emotional reaction to his patient, a reaction that is caused by the analyst's own pathology in which the analyst's countertransference is an interference. Gradually, analysts became aware that their countertransference could be a useful source of information about the patient. In 1950, Heimann – Bion was in supervision with her at the time – wrote an important paper in which she claimed that countertransference is "an instrument of research into the patient's unconscious" and she referred to countertransference as the patient's "creation". Analysts began to think increasingly about their own feelings in order to discover the aspects of the patient that had been projected into them.

Klein was not happy with the degree of interest that analysts were taking in the examination of their own feelings. In her seminars on technique, given in 1958, she said the following:

> I have never found that the counter-transference has helped me to understand my patient better; but, if I may put it like this, I have found that it has helped me to understand myself better … In Berlin there was a saying, "if you feel like that about your patient, then go in a corner and think out carefully what is wrong with you".
>
> (quoted in Steiner, 2017, p. 103)

Gammill (1989) wrote that he thought Klein was in agreement with the use being made of countertransference feelings but that she thought the analyst needed to detect other "evidence demonstrable to the patient of the theme or feelings aroused". I remember Hannah Segal telling me how important it was to find corroborative evidence from the patient's speech or dreams to any countertransference feelings that I might have; she thought that countertransference feelings alone were not enough information on which to base an interpretation. In a footnote to his paper, Gammill quotes a letter from Joseph who queried what he had written regarding Klein's acceptance of the use of countertransference:

> I believe she thought that many people used this term to cover an analyst's lack of understanding of his own difficulties ...
>
> In this connection, Melanie Klein told me about a young unmarried woman whose difficulty was that the child in analysis often sat on her lap. Finally, this situation became clear in a supervisory session when the young woman said spontaneously: "Oh! Mrs. Klein he is so adorable that I wish he were my child."
>
> (Gammill, 1989, p. 3)

This confirms the suggestion that Klein feared that analysts were failing to distinguish between their own feelings and feelings coming from the patient.

Klein acknowledged that patients push feelings into their analysts but she thought that the analyst should be aware of the pressure from the patient and resist it:

> One is aware that the patient is pushing something into me and it depends on me whether I let him push it into me. I mean, there are two of us here, he pushes it into me, but I won't have it pushed into me. I would rather consider what he is doing at that moment when he is pushing.
>
> (Klein in Steiner, 2017, p. 105)

It is not only the patient who gets into the analyst, the analyst gets into the patient. Klein wrote that, as well as being projected into, she projected herself into her patient in order to understand him, but 'up to a point'. I think that 'up to a point' is the crux of Klein's argument; allow the patient's projections in, but only up to a point.

It is well understood by analysts that it is important to separate out what belongs to who and that the analyst needs to do her best to clarify which feelings belong to her and which come from the patient. In a seminal paper on this issue, Money-Kyrle (1956) described the process of introjecting and identifying with the patient's projection before reprojecting it out in the form of an interpretation. He outlined various difficulties; for example, occasions on which the analyst introjects an aspect of the patient that he has not yet understood in himself, and he gave an example of teasing out his own incompetence – something that he knew about – from the incompetence that had been projected into him.

In a more recent paper, Irma Brenman Pick (1985) put forward the idea that the patient projects into a particular aspect of you. Significantly also, she emphasized the importance of the analyst working through her feelings in the session with the patient. Her ideas draw attention to the analyst's live experience of difficult feelings and make the point that it is the analyst's capacity to experience and manage these difficult feelings that gives the patient the opportunity to take in a strengthening capacity from the analyst. As you can see, this is in line with Bion's idea of the need for an object with sufficient strength to contain the projections. The analyst, like the mother, takes in a difficult experience, works it through and returns an understanding to the patient. It seems to me that this also has elements of Klein's idea that the patient pushes something in, but up to a point. The analyst does not get mixed up with her patient, or rather gets mixed up but then separates out and works on managing the feelings – her own and those of her patient – that are stirred up in her. The idea that the patient explores his feelings by projecting them into the analyst also has links to Klein's idea of the epistemophilic instinct – a drive to get in and know.

For Brenman Pick, an understanding that does not contain an emotional experience but is an understanding that is solely intellectual will not contain the depth necessary for change, a point also made by Klein. Whereas if the patient has the experience of the analyst having to struggle with coming to terms with difficult feelings or of making sense of troubling thoughts, the patient senses that the analyst has taken something in from them. In Brenman Pick's view, an infant is not just hungry for food, he is also hungry for someone who is able to know how he feels.

It is inevitable that at times mothers become overwhelmed by their infants and that at times psychotherapists and analysts become overwhelmed by their patients. A mother may become enormously anxious or furious and she will need someone else, for example a father, a grandparent or a friend, to come in and help her with her feelings and with the infant. Similarly, analysts need colleagues or supervisors to help them bear the anxiety or confusion or rage that patients can make them feel. Sometimes too the patient's disturbance may be too great for an individual analyst to manage and the patient will need a stronger container such as a case manager, medication or an institution.

Links with the Past

Although Klein was severely criticized in her time for too great a focus on the transference, she strongly conveyed in her lectures and seminars in the 1930s and 1940s that she thought that it was important for the analyst to link transference interpretations to the past; to connect what is going on with the patient now, to what happened to them in the past. Klein became concerned about the increasing focus that analysts gave to the present in their sessions with patients, along with a tendency to neglect making the connection between the present and the patient's history:

> In recent years the importance of transference to be gathered from the unconscious, as well as from conscious material has been recognised, but the old concept that transference means a repetition from the past seems to have correspondingly diminished. One hears again and again the expression of the "here and now" laying the whole emphasis on what the patient experiences towards the analyst and leaves out the links with the past ... we must be aware that analysing the relations of the present to the analyst both from conscious

and unconscious material does not serve its purpose if we are not able, step by step, to link it with the earliest emotions and relations.

(From MK Archive PP/KLE D17 in Spillius, 2007, p. 93)

Despite Klein's dismay, the focus on the transference and in particular the minutiae of the interaction between the analyst and patient in the here and now has continued. Bion's (1976) paper "Notes on memory and desire" could be understood as an instruction that the analyst remember nothing about the patient, in fact to clear her mind of what she already knows. While this would be an extreme position to take, Bion's is an important point as he draws attention to the danger, one that had been pointed out by Freud, of the analyst "never finding anything but what he already knows" (Freud, 1912b, p. 112). Prior knowledge can interfere with learning something new, it can colour every perception and close down thinking. What we know about the patient and what we know about theory needs to be in the back of our minds rather the front.

Joseph strongly advocated working with the fine detail of the immediate projective and introjective identifications in the transference. She had no doubt that in attending to the here and now, she was also attending to her patient's history:

I am not reconstructing my patient's history and past from what I am being or have been told, the history is reconstructing itself. I am being asked to play particular roles in the reconstruction but my task is to try to be aware of the ways I am being asked to act and to interpret accordingly, not merely to fit into the role.

(Joseph, 1996, unpublished)

More recently, in his paper "The illumination of history" Feldman (2007) showed the way in which the patient's history lives on in the internal object relationships. Like Joseph his conviction is that understanding the current object relationships leads to changes in the relationships between the internal objects. Feldman described how, as understanding emerges in the transference, memories from the past emerge into consciousness, the ego becomes strengthened, distortions are given up and the present no longer continues to repeat the past.

> This can allow the patient to achieve a greater sense of the presence of an organic history with meanings and connections. I suggest this process comes about through the analytical process modifying the internal forces that have interfered, and continue to interfere, with the patient's own capacity to make connections, to discover and tolerate the meaning of what emerges.
>
> (Feldman, 2007, p. 623)

Joseph (1996) and Feldman's (2007) way of working is not easy; it is difficult to recognize what is going on in the immediate here and now – the analyst is not always aware of the feelings that she has and may only realize what she feels when she sees how she is behaving. An analyst may have a particular feeling towards her patient but be unaware until it is seen by colleagues when she discusses her case in a seminar or with a supervisor. Sometimes the analyst realizes from her own behaviour when she finds herself doing something that she would not usually do. But it is more difficult to notice oneself doing something that is not unusual; difficult too, for example, when a patient makes us feel good about ourselves and makes us feel helpful – such feelings might mistakenly lead us to think we have nothing to question. For example, the patient may project into the analyst's motherly aspect. What I mean by this is that the patient may project all or much of his own capacity to take care into the analyst where it links with the analyst's own wish to be caring and helpful.

It is more than a feeling that is projected, it is a particular object relationship – a good mother–infant relationship but too good to be true and one that may infantalize the patient. Being motherly can go wrong if it is taken too far or goes on for two long and interferes with the patient's development of his own capacity to take care of himself. The analyst's aim is for the patient to develop and stand on his own two feet. We are not with our patients all the time nor are we going to be around for ever.

Our aim as described by Eric Brenman is for the patient to recover his own lost good objects and find within himself a supporting strength and capacity to manage life (Brenman, 2006).

Clinical Example

I will bring an example from a patient for whom my helpfulness, while it may have been necessary at the start, fitted into a particular object relationship that protected the patient from feelings of humiliation. When Mrs C first came to see me, she cried but she had no idea what was upsetting her. Her speech was broken up so that it was very difficult for me to piece together the meaning of her incomplete sentences and words. My patient had been looked after by many different people during her childhood. She told me that if she became attached to anyone they were sent away.

In a similar way I thought that Mrs C avoided contact with her feelings; her emotional self was split up, fragmented and sent away, and it ended up scattered around in other people. Mrs C was very active on behalf of these others who she felt had little capacity to control or to care for themselves and who needed her to look after them; she felt under great pressure to race all over the place in response to their needs. For quite a long period I was included in the group of people demanding her attention and she was far more aware of her activity in relation to me, than in her passivity in helping me to understand her. She found the sessions meaningless, boring and without value.

Mrs C was concerned about others but her concern for herself was located in me. I felt that she needed me to work hard on her behalf, to pick up the pieces of what she said, collect the parts of her from wherever they were now located, to link them together and to connect my and her thoughts and her feelings. I did not see that I was being active on her behalf and that I was behaving in the way that she did when she ran around on behalf of all those whom she looked after. If the meaning that I constructed made sense to her, it was sometimes possible for me to make emotional contact with her, and this meant that gradually I became valued as someone who could sort things out. Slowly she allowed herself to have feelings. She still far preferred to suffer virtuously than be selfish, greedy or aggressive, but she was able to recover, to some extent, some of these aspects of herself that I thought she needed in order to grow and protect herself.

Gradually I realized that Mrs C could speak more clearly and connect her ideas together better than she had wanted me to know; I put this to her. Her immediate reaction was defensive, but in the following session she was more coherent and thoughtful than usual. She told me that she was very afraid of how she would manage without me in the impending holiday, and said "a funny thing happened, the council told us that we had to sort out our rubbish and said that the collectors would only take away what was sorted out". I thought that she had taken my words as saying to her "you cannot leave me to do all the work of making sense of what you say, you have to sort out what you can yourself", and so I put this to her, she agreed and went on to tell me a dream:

> *We were going for the weekend to stay with William. I didn't know the way and then Marina, his wife, came down the drive and so I followed her. There were other people and they also followed her and we went into the house. There was a door, which Marina changed into a window to let in light, and then William came in and he had a lot of children with him. He had brought them back from his travels, you know he goes on these expeditions. We were talking about it and I did not know the difference between the Arctic and the Antarctic and we were talking to the children. Then he fed them and they were very hungry and they changed into animals and the food was running out and so he got some more, a leg of pork or ham. It was on a spit and he was anxious that it would not be cooked fast enough. The children had not been like animals before.*

Mrs C had an association to a man on TV licking milk out of a saucer, eating like a cat – she had found it very disturbing. It had made her feel uncomfortable to see him doing something so humiliating. There are aspects of this dream that I do not understand, but I think that it is possible to see that the analysis, like the window in the dream, shed some light on what happened between us when I brought parts of Mrs C in from the cold and fed her with my attention and understanding; it made her hungry for more (and I think anxious too about the time that was running out before the holiday) but a 'viewer' her looked down on her with disgust at what she considered to be an animal side of herself. I told Mrs C that I thought that she felt that being hungry turned her into an animal, and that taking food from me, in fact having good feelings towards me and wanting something from me, made her feel very uncomfortable, as though she was involved in something disgusting and degrading. I went on to say that she is much more comfortable with a version of me as the rubbish collector. She replied "I don't think it has changed, I still feel it is humiliating to be hungry".

I think that my running about picking up ideas about Mrs C and putting them together put me in the place of devalued inferior rubbish collector – the sessions were felt to be boring and of no value. I think that this object relationship, in which she was the superior one, defended her against feelings of loss. What loss is there at the departure of an inferior person who sorts out and clears up the mess and picks up the pieces when another one can be found to take her place? Mrs C was defended against the pain of an object relationship in which she might feel dependent on someone else of value who might leave her. It was only when I realized that I was doing more for Mrs C than she needed, and that she could make less of a mess, could make sense of things herself and speak clearly, was it possible to grasp that fear of humiliation prevented her from being able to acknowledge her needs and that this in turn prevented her from being able to develop and make full use of her capacities to think and talk. As you can see, Mrs C's history was played out in the transference–countertransference relationship with me.

Some Concluding Thoughts

Klein's awareness of the importance of negative feelings remains a significant guiding principle for analysts who are trained in the Kleinian tradition, but aggression is not stressed in the way that it was in the early papers of some Kleinian authors of the 1950s and 1960s. Spillius referred to these papers as "a step backwards from the work of Klein herself, especially from her later work" (Spillius, 2007, p. 50). Klein was dismayed by the way in which her ideas were taken up and is recorded as having said in a discussion with young colleagues in 1958:

> There was a time when I felt very badly because my work on bringing out the problem of aggression [led to the result] that there was nothing but aggression. [I] was quite despairing. Whatever I heard in seminars, in the Society, it all was aggression, aggression, aggression … the point is that aggression can only be tolerated [when it is] modified, mitigated if we are able to bring out the capacity for love.
>
> (quoted in Spillius, 2007, p. 81)

Analysts aim to keep a close eye on the interplay between their comments, their patient's response and their own responses and to be aware of what is being enacted in the session. It is recognized that live feelings are necessary for change and that talking about what is going on now has an emotional impact and makes emotional rather than solely intellectual sense. The analyst wants the patient to understand that what she says is more than just an idea and that what is being spoken about is a living part of him that is real, live now and has an impact on how the patient is in the world. At the same time, the analyst wants the patient to be able to take in what she says, and this can be difficult. Live feelings can be painful, and patients will frequently back away from them into the protective structure of their defences. Steiner has drawn attention to the shame experienced by the patient at being seen by the analyst and more recently to the humiliating aspects of the dynamic in the analytic situation in which the patient repeatedly suffers the experience of being the one without the power (Steiner, 2020). An experience that can lead the patient to feel that the analyst's main motive is to enjoy the exercise of power.

Analysts interpret the transference in the here and now and sometimes may refer solely to an intrapsychic conflict within the patient and they vary in the degree to which they make links to their patient's history. Priscilla Roth (2001) has set out with great clarity the different levels at which we interpret: at the level of a figure from the patient's past, at the level of the figure from the past representing the patient's thoughts and feelings about the analyst and, lastly, two levels in which those thoughts and feelings are part of an enactment that is taking place in the immediacy of the analysis. Analysts are likely to interpret at all different levels during the course of an analysis, and even during the course of a session.

References

Abram, J. & Hinshelwood, R. D. (2018) *The Clinical Paradigms of Melanie Klein and Donald Winnicott*. London: Routledge.

Bion, W. R. (1957) On arrogance, presented at the Twentieth International Psycho-Analytic Congress, Paris; reprinted in *International Journal of Psycho-Analysis*, 39: 144–146 (1958).

Bion, W. R. (1959) Attacks on linking, *International Journal of Psycho-Analysis*, 40: 308–315.

Bion, W. R. (1967) Notes on memory and desire, *The Psychoanalysis Forum*, 2: 272, 279–280.

Brenman, E. (2006) 'The recovery of the good object relationship: The conflict with the superego, in *Recovery of the Lost Good Object*. London: Routledge, pp. 94–106.

Brenman Pick, I. (1985) Working through in the countertransference. *International Journal of Psycho-Analysis*, 66: 157–166.

Feldman, M. (2007) The illumination of history. *International Journal of Psycho-Analysis*, 88: 609–625.

Freud, S. (1912a) The dynamics of transference, *S.E.* 12: 97–108. London: Hogarth.

Freud, S. (1912b) Recommendations to physicians practising psychoanalysis, *S.E.* 12: 109–120. London: Hogarth.

Freud, S. (1950) Project for a scientific psychology, *S.E.* 1: 295–346. London: Hogarth.

Gammill, J. (1989) Some personal reflections of Melanie Klein, *Melanie Klein and Object Relations*, 7(2).

Heimann, P. (1950) On counter-transference. *International Journal of Psycho-Analysis*, 31: 71–84.

Joseph, B. (1996) Uses of the past in the psychoanalytic process. Unpublished manuscript quoted in Feldman (2007).

Klein, M. (1952) The origins of the transference, in *The Writings of Melanie Klein*, vol. 3. London: Hogarth Press, pp. 48–56.

Klein, M. (1957) Envy and gratitude, in *The Writings of Melanie Klein*, vol. 3. London: Hogarth Press, pp. 176–235.

Klein, M. (1959) Our adult world and its roots in infancy, in *The Writings of Melanie Klein* Vol. 3. London: Hogarth Press, pp. 247–263.

Klein, M. (1963) On the sense of loneliness, in *The Writings of Melanie Klein*, vol. 3. London: Hogarth Press, pp. 300–313.

Mawson, C. (2018) The projective process and the two positions today, in P. Garvey & K. Long (eds.), *The Klein Tradition*. London: Routledge, pp. 185–197.

Money-Kyrle, R. E. (1956) Normal counter-transference and some of its deviations. *International Journal of Psycho-Analysis*, 37: 360–366.

Roth, P, (2001). Mapping the landscape: Levels of transference interpretation, *International Journal of Psycho-Analysis*, 82: 533–545.

Spillius, E. (2007) *Encounters with Melanie Klein: Selected Papers of Elizabeth Spillius*. P. Roth & R. Rusbridger (eds.). London: Routledge.

Steiner, J. (ed.) (2017) *Lectures on Technique by Melanie Klein*. London: Routledge.

Steiner, J. (2020) *Illusion, Disillusion, and Irony in Psychoanalysis*. London: Routledge.

Index

Roth, Priscilla, 105–106
Rustin, Margaret, 33

sadism, 12, 76
  oral, 19, 20, 25
Sandler, Joseph, 14
schizophrenia, 48
Schmideberg, Melitta (daughter),
  7, 8, 13, 15, 47
Schreber, Daniel Paul, 48
Segal, Hanna, 49, 51, 66, 68,
  86–87, 97
separation, 59, 67
  case material, 83, 84
sexuality. *See* Oedipus complex;
  psychosexual stages
social issues. *See under* defences
Sodre, Ignes, 67
Sohn, Leslie, 49
Spillius, Elizabeth. B., 104–105
splitting, 42, 43, 50, 51
  awareness of the split, 45
  case material, 45–46, 83
  Freud on, 45
  in groups, 50
  Klein on, 37–39, 41, 47, 55,
    76–77, 93
  nature of, 42
  paranoid-schizoid position and,
    37, 46, 55
  projection and, 37–41
  projective identification and,
    38, 39
  psychosis and, 41, 46–48
  Rosenfeld on, 41, 48, 77
  superego and, 76–77
  trauma and, 67–68
  types of, 45–46, 76–77
    binary, 37–38, 41, 46, 47
    fragmentary, 46–48. *See also*
      fragmentation
    horizontal vs. vertical, 43

Steiner, John, 29, 46, 69, 70,
  78, 105
Strachey, Alix, 10
Strachey, James, 32
suicide, 78, 84, 85
superego, 86, 87
  abnormal, 87
  destructive, 25, 75–78, 82
    case material, 79. *See also*
      cases: Mrs B
  early, 24–25, 75
  Freud on, 25, 63, 74, 75
  introjects and, 41, 75
  modification of, 75–78
    negative transference and,
      31–32
  and Oedipus complex, 25, 75
  origin, 75
  overview of concept of, 74–75
  Rosenfeld on, 77, 78
  splitting and, 76–77
  See also guilt
symbolic equation, 68
symbolism, 29
  moving from the concrete to the
    symbolic, 66–68

transference, 100
  Freud on, 30, 90
  Klein on, 9, 29–31, 90, 99–100
  negative, and modification of
    superego, 31–32
transference interpretation, 29, 32,
  105–106
  links with the past, 99–102
trauma, 67–68

Winnicott, Donald W., 15, 93
  Klein and, 15, 16, 28, 93–94
wish fulfillment. *See* hallucination
Wittgenstein, Ludwig, 33
World War II, 12, 50